United States Government Accountability Office

Report to Congressional Addressees

I0448461

February 2013

AFGHANISTAN

Key Oversight Issues

GAO
Accountability * Integrity * Reliability

GAO-13-218SP

Contents

Figures

Abbreviations

AFSA	Afghanistan Freedom Support Act
AIF	Afghanistan Infrastructure Fund
ANA	Afghan National Army
ANP	Afghan National Police
ANSF	Afghan National Security Forces
APPF	Afghan Public Protection Force
ASFF	Afghan Security Forces Fund
CENTCOM	U.S. Central Command

CERP	Commander's Emergency Response Program
DA	Development Assistance
DOD	Department of Defense
DOD CN	Department of Defense Drug Interdiction and Counter-Drug Activities
DOJ	Department of Justice
ERMA	Emergency Refugee and Migration Assistance
ESF	Economic Support Fund
FMF	Foreign Military Financing
GDP	Gross Domestic Product
GHCS	Global Health and Child Survival
IDA	International Disaster Assistance
IMET	International Military Education and Training
IMF	International Monetary Fund
INCLE	International Narcotics Control and Law Enforcement
ISAF	International Security Assistance Force
MNNA	Major Non-NATO Ally
MRA	Migration and Refugee Assistance
NADR	Nonproliferation, Antiterrorism, Demining, and Related Programs
NATO	North Atlantic Treaty Organization
NDAA	National Defense Authorization Act
OPLAN	Operational Plan
PKO	Voluntary Peacekeeping
PMP	Performance Management Plan
PSC	Private security contractor
RC	Regional Command
SHAPE	Supreme Headquarters of the Allied Powers Europe
SIGAR	Special Inspector General for Afghanistan Reconstruction
State	Department of State
TFBSO	Task Force for Business and Stability Operations
UN	United Nations
USAID	U.S. Agency for International Development
USFOR-A	U.S. Forces-Afghanistan

February 11, 2013

Congressional Addressees:

The U.S. strategic goal for Afghanistan is to defeat and prevent the return of al Qaeda and its affiliates. Since fiscal year 2002, U.S. costs reported for U.S. military, U.S. diplomatic, and reconstruction and relief operations in Afghanistan have been over $500 billion.[1] Given U.S. strategic goals and the level of U.S. resources expected to support Afghanistan in the future, we have identified a number of key issues for the 113th Congress to consider in developing oversight agendas and determining the way forward in Afghanistan. Significant oversight will be needed to help ensure visibility over the cost and progress of these efforts. The enclosures, based on existing GAO work, suggest specific areas for oversight on the following topics:

- *Afghanistan's security environment.* Afghanistan's security situation remains volatile in part due to an increase in insider attacks.

- *Transition of lead security to Afghan security forces.* The security transition is under way, and international forces are shifting to an advise-and-assist mission.

- *Future cost and sustainability of Afghan security forces.* A shortfall currently exists in Afghan domestic revenue and international commitments to cover the anticipated costs of Afghan security forces, and despite past recommendations and a congressional mandate, the Department of Defense (DOD) has not routinely provided long-term cost estimates for sustaining those forces.

- *DOD planning for the drawdown of equipment in Afghanistan.* DOD has applied some lessons learned from Iraq to its planning and has

---

[1]We reviewed estimates developed by the Congressional Research Service and Special Inspector General for Afghanistan Reconstruction, as well as obligations data provided by DOD and allotment data provided by the Departments of Justice and State. While allotment data are available for U.S. reconstruction and relief efforts in Afghanistan, specific funding figures of U.S. military operations in Afghanistan do not exist because funding provided to DOD for military operations is generally appropriated by operation, not country. Specifically, DOD received funding for Operation Enduring Freedom, which includes Afghanistan.

taken several steps to prepare for the drawdown in Afghanistan, but has not fully considered the costs and benefits of returning excess equipment.

- *Afghanistan's donor dependence.* Afghanistan's domestic revenues do not cover its total public expenditures, over 90 percent of which are covered by the United States and international partners. The international community has pledged its continued support.

- *Oversight and accountability of U.S. funds to support Afghanistan.* The United States continues to take steps to improve Afghanistan's financial management capacity, as well as the accountability of U.S. direct assistance.

- *Oversight and streamlining of development assistance to Afghanistan.* Oversight of U.S. programmatic funds has been enhanced, but U.S. development efforts in Afghanistan could benefit from a shared database.

- *Oversight of U.S. contracts in Afghanistan.* Contract management and contractor vetting require continued attention.

- *Planning for the future U.S. presence in Afghanistan.* The military to civilian-led transition in Iraq could offer lessons for similar efforts in Afghanistan as the United States plans for five diplomatic sites and the future U.S. military presence is under negotiations.

Background

The Islamic Republic of Afghanistan is a mountainous, land-locked, and economically poor country of over 30 million ethnically diverse people located in central Asia. (See fig. 1 for an interactive geopolitical map of Afghanistan.)

Figure 1: Interactive Geopolitical Map of Afghanistan

Directions:

[Click ✈] on the buttons to view more information.

| Geopolitical map | Ethnic map | Access map |

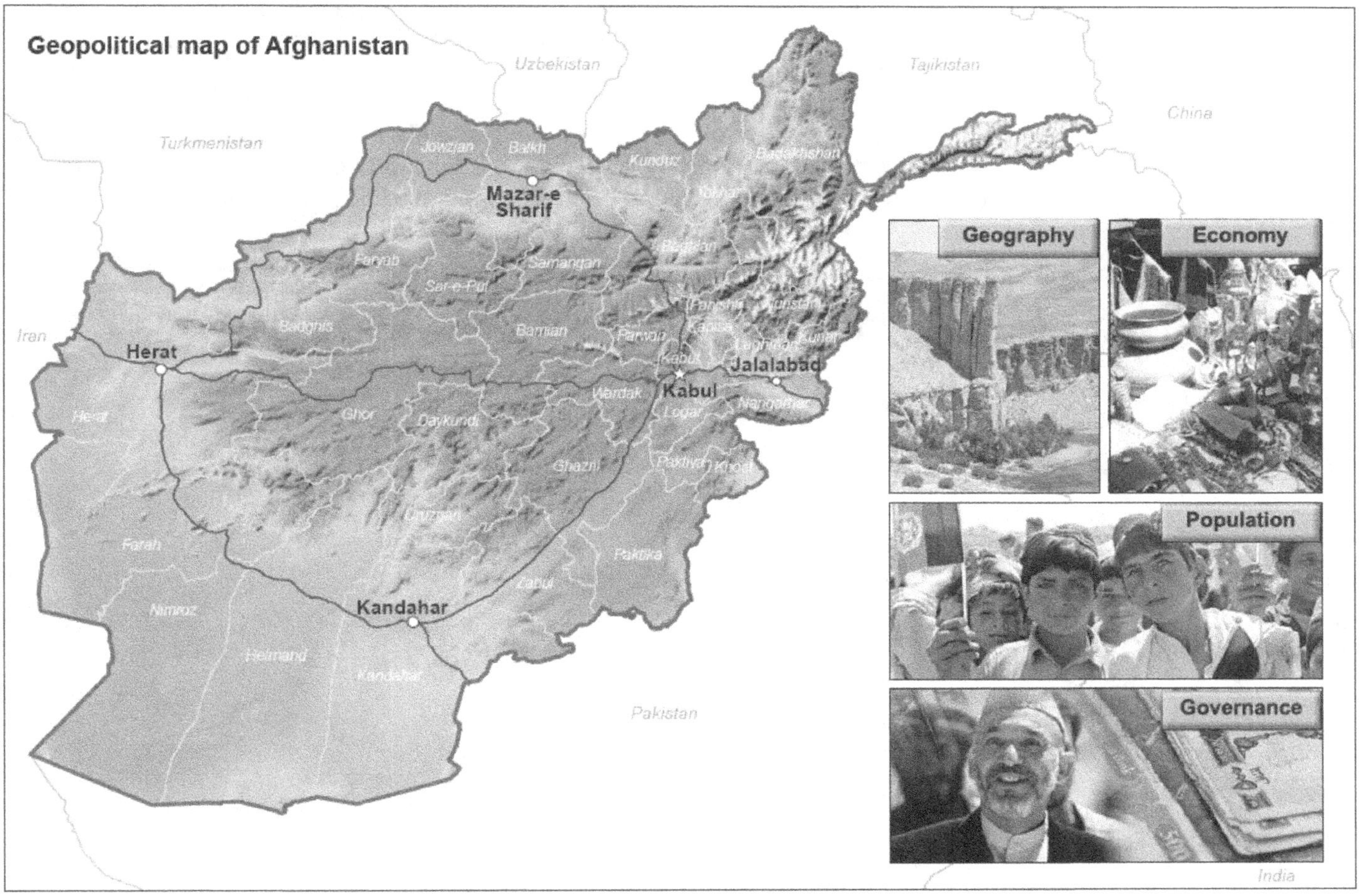

Geopolitical map of Afghanistan

Uzbekistan

Tajikistan

China

Turkmenistan

Jowzjan   Balkh

Kunduz   Badakhshan

Mazar-e Sharif

Takhar

Faryab   Samangan

Sar-e-Pul   Baghlan

Iran

Badghis

Bamian   Parwan   Kapisa   Nuristan

Kabul   Laghman   Kunar

Herat   **Jalalabad**

Herat   Wardak   **Kabul**   Nangarhar

Logar

Ghor   Daykundi

Ghazni   Paktiya/khost

Farah   Uruzgan

Paktika

Zabul

Nimroz   **Kandahar**

Pakistan

Helmand

Kandahar

India

Geography

Economy

Population

Governance

Source: Central Intelligence Agency, *The World Factbook*, and Government of Afghanistan, *National Risk and Vulnerability Assessment 2007/2008: A Profile of Afghanistan*; Map Resources (map); Department of Defense and Central Intelligence Agency (photos).

Print instructions

• Click to make view needed visible. In the "Print" dialog box, choose "current view," then "OK." Repeat for each view.
• A print version of this graphic is also available in appendices I, II and III.

Recent U.S.-Afghan Events

In June 2011, the President announced that after nearly a decade of conflict in Afghanistan, U.S. combat troops would be withdrawn in 2014. The President also announced that the United States would remain committed to supporting the development of a sovereign Afghanistan. In May 2012, the United States signed the Enduring Strategic Partnership Agreement with Afghanistan, outlining the goals for the future bilateral relationship, and in November 2012, the two nations began negotiations on a future bilateral security agreement that would govern any future role for U.S. military forces. It is possible that some U.S. forces would remain in Afghanistan to advise or assist the Afghan government after 2014; however, no decisions have yet been made. U.S. forces in Afghanistan have begun to draw down from an estimated high of 99,800 in March 2011 to approximately 66,000 in December 2012 and shift their role from carrying out combat operations to advising and assisting Afghan forces while transitioning lead security responsibilities to Afghan forces. Afghanistan is scheduled to hold presidential elections in April 2014. According to Department of State (State) officials, the 2014 election will be the crucial test of Afghanistan's political transition. (See fig. 2 for a time line of selected events and U.S. troop levels in Afghanistan.)

Figure 2: Time Line of Selected Events and U.S. Troop Levels in Afghanistan, 2001-2012

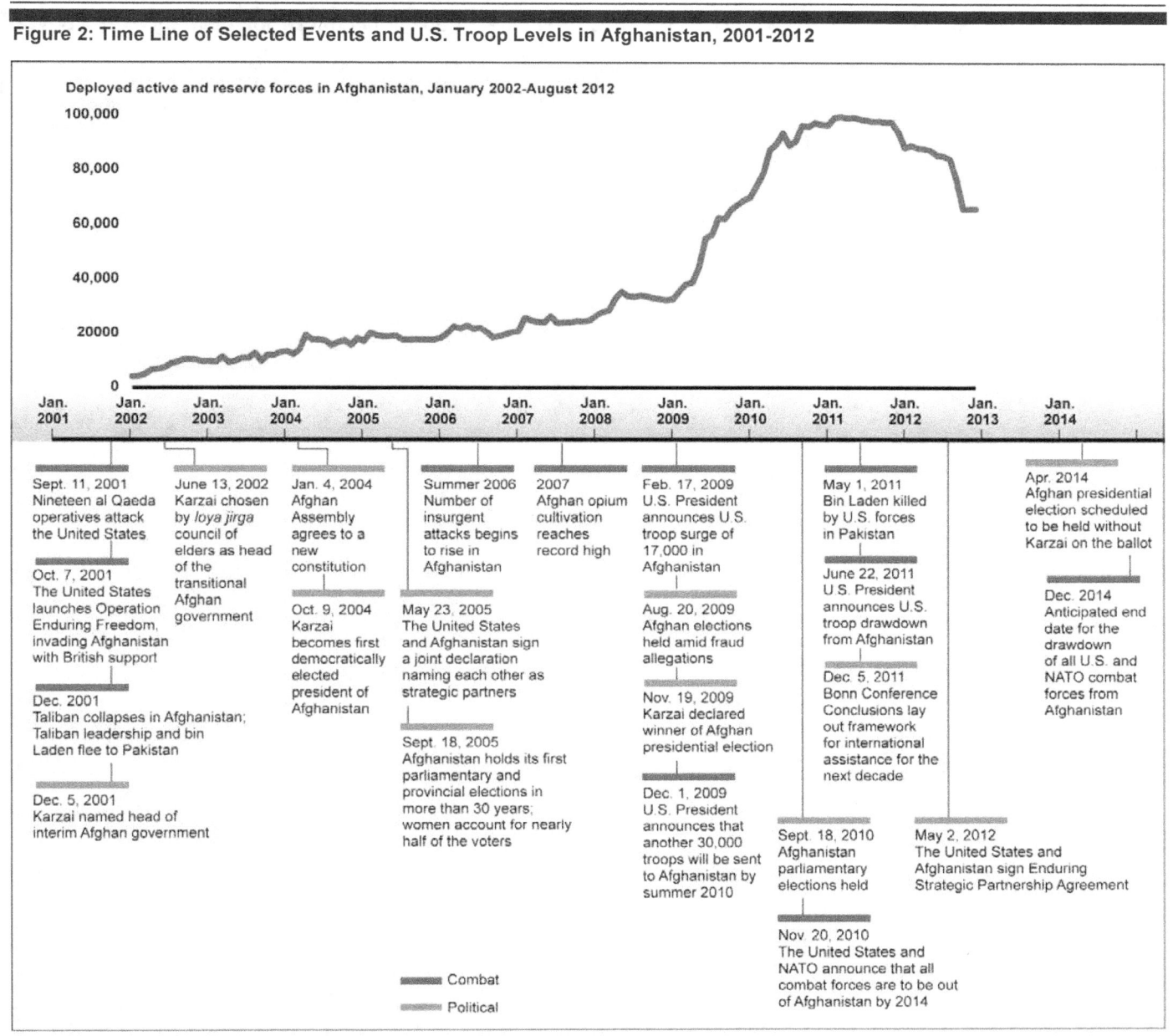

Deployed active and reserve forces in Afghanistan, January 2002-August 2012

Sept. 11, 2001
Nineteen al Qaeda operatives attack the United States

Oct. 7, 2001
The United States launches Operation Enduring Freedom, invading Afghanistan with British support

Dec. 2001
Taliban collapses in Afghanistan; Taliban leadership and bin Laden flee to Pakistan

Dec. 5, 2001
Karzai named head of interim Afghan government

June 13, 2002
Karzai chosen by *loya jirga* council of elders as head of the transitional Afghan government

Jan. 4, 2004
Afghan Assembly agrees to a new constitution

Oct. 9, 2004
Karzai becomes first democratically elected president of Afghanistan

Summer 2006
Number of insurgent attacks begins to rise in Afghanistan

May 23, 2005
The United States and Afghanistan sign a joint declaration naming each other as strategic partners

Sept. 18, 2005
Afghanistan holds its first parliamentary and provincial elections in more than 30 years; women account for nearly half of the voters

2007
Afghan opium cultivation reaches record high

Feb. 17, 2009
U.S. President announces U.S. troop surge of 17,000 in Afghanistan

Aug. 20, 2009
Afghan elections held amid fraud allegations

Nov. 19, 2009
Karzai declared winner of Afghan presidential election

Dec. 1, 2009
U.S. President announces that another 30,000 troops will be sent to Afghanistan by summer 2010

May 1, 2011
Bin Laden killed by U.S. forces in Pakistan

June 22, 2011
U.S. President announces U.S. troop drawdown from Afghanistan

Dec. 5, 2011
Bonn Conference Conclusions lay out framework for international assistance for the next decade

Sept. 18, 2010
Afghanistan parliamentary elections held

Nov. 20, 2010
The United States and NATO announce that all combat forces are to be out of Afghanistan by 2014

May 2, 2012
The United States and Afghanistan sign Enduring Strategic Partnership Agreement

Apr. 2014
Afghan presidential election scheduled to be held without Karzai on the ballot

Dec. 2014
Anticipated end date for the drawdown of all U.S. and NATO combat forces from Afghanistan

Combat
Political

Sources: Congressional Research Service (active and reserve troop data); White House, DOD, State, Government of Afghanistan, United Nations, North Atlantic Treaty Organization, and other open-source material (timeline dates and events).

Strategic Framework for U.S. Efforts in Afghanistan

The U.S. strategic goal for Afghanistan is to disrupt, dismantle, and defeat al Qaeda and prevent its return to Afghanistan and Pakistan. Specific objectives in Afghanistan in support of this goal are to (1) deny safe haven to al Qaeda and (2) deny the Taliban the ability to overthrow the Afghan government.[2] (See fig. 3 for a description of key strategies and plans that collectively guide U.S. efforts in Afghanistan.)

---

[2]The U.S. strategic goals for Afghanistan were recently changed from those that appeared in the October 2012 U.S. Civil-Military Strategic Framework for Afghanistan. The goals as they appeared in October 2012 were to (1) disrupt, dismantle, and defeat al Qaeda and its affiliates and prevent their return to Afghanistan; and (2) build a partnership with the Afghan people that ensures that the United States will be able to continue to target terrorists and support a sovereign Afghan government.

Figure 3: Framework for U.S. Efforts in Afghanistan

Directions: 🖱 Mouseover text to view more information.

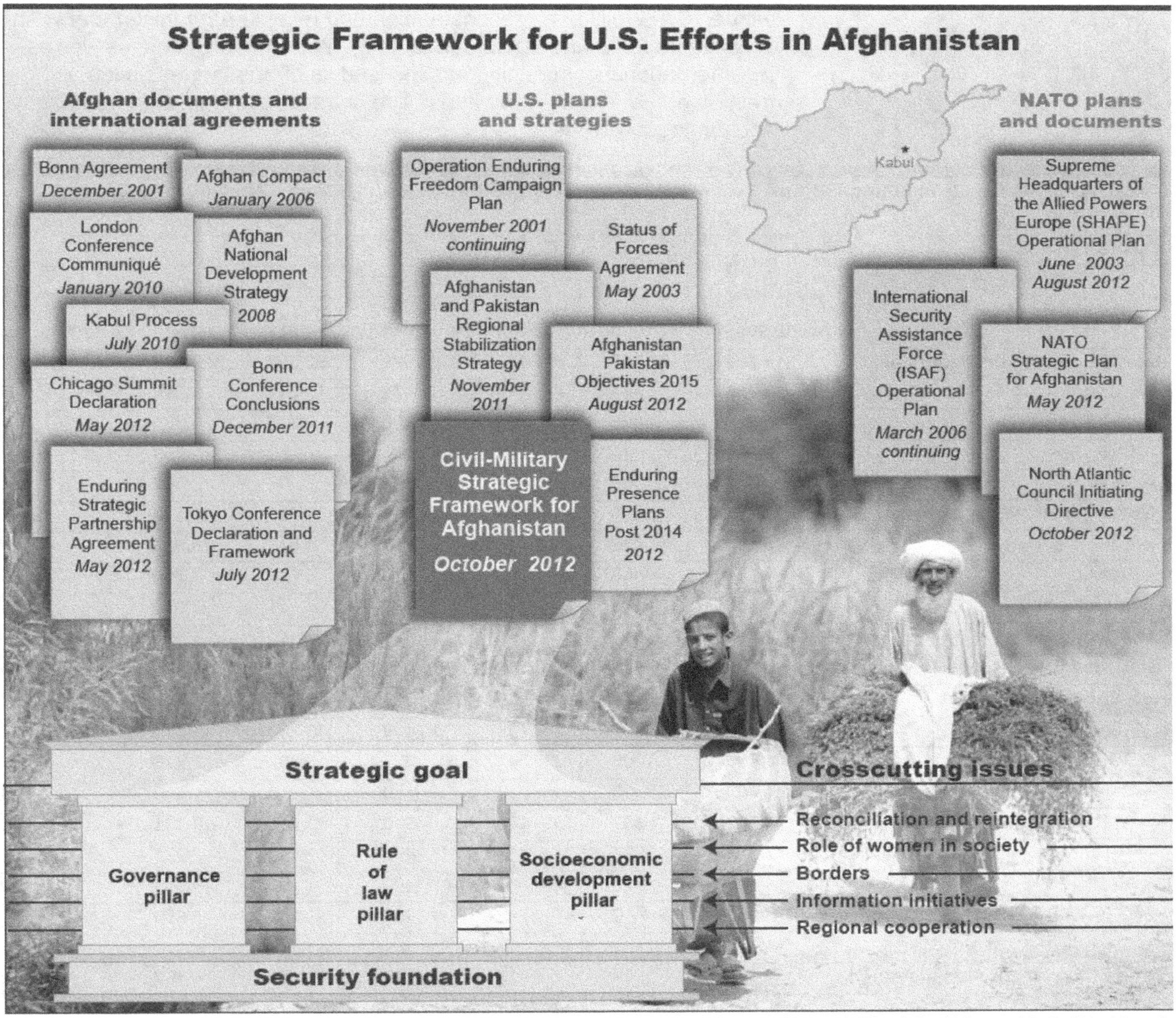

Strategic Framework for U.S. Efforts in Afghanistan

Afghan documents and international agreements

Bonn Agreement
December 2001

Afghan Compact
January 2006

London Conference Communiqué
January 2010

Afghan National Development Strategy
2008

Kabul Process
July 2010

Chicago Summit Declaration
May 2012

Bonn Conference Conclusions
December 2011

Enduring Strategic Partnership Agreement
May 2012

Tokyo Conference Declaration and Framework
July 2012

U.S. plans and strategies

Operation Enduring Freedom Campaign Plan
November 2001 continuing

Status of Forces Agreement
May 2003

Afghanistan and Pakistan Regional Stabilization Strategy
November 2011

Afghanistan Pakistan Objectives 2015
August 2012

Civil-Military Strategic Framework for Afghanistan
October 2012

Enduring Presence Plans Post 2014
2012

Kabul

NATO plans and documents

Supreme Headquarters of the Allied Powers Europe (SHAPE) Operational Plan
June 2003 August 2012

International Security Assistance Force (ISAF) Operational Plan
March 2006 continuing

NATO Strategic Plan for Afghanistan
May 2012

North Atlantic Council Initiating Directive
October 2012

Strategic goal

Crosscutting issues

| Governance pillar | Rule of law pillar | Socioeconomic development pillar |

Reconciliation and reintegration
Role of women in society
Borders
Information initiatives
Regional cooperation

Security foundation

Source: Department of Defense, Department of State, U.S. Mission to NATO, U.S. Special Representative for Afghanistan and Pakistan, U.S. Central Command, U.S. Agency for International Development, UN, and government of Afghanistan documents; Department of Defense (photo); Map Resources (map).

 **Print instructions** | • A print version of this graphic is also available in appendices IV and V.

Funding for U.S. Efforts in Afghanistan

As of September 30, 2012, DOD had reported obligations of about $440 billion for Operation Enduring Freedom from September 2001 through the end of fiscal year 2012. U.S. agencies allotted $6.6 billion for diplomatic operations between fiscal years 2002 and 2012. U.S. agencies also allotted $79.7 billion for reconstruction and relief in Afghanistan between fiscal years 2002 and 2012 (see table 1). The United States, as well as the international community, has focused its efforts in areas such as training of the Afghan army and police, infrastructure development, and economic growth.

Table 1: U.S. Allotments to Support Afghan Reconstruction and Relief by Category and Selected Accounts, Fiscal Years 2002-2013

Dollars in millions

	Fiscal years					2002-2012 Total	2013 Request
	2002-2008	2009	2010	2011	2012		
International Affairs Programs	**$11,596**	**$2,813**	**$4,179**	**$2,689**	**$2,308**	**$23,586**	**$2,570**
Security[a]	**3,186**	**534**	**648**	**471**	**391**	**5,229**	**656**
—INCLE	1,787	484	589	400	324	3,584	600
—FMF	1,059	0	0	0	0	1,059	0
—Other	340	50	59	71	67	587	56
Governance and development[b]	**6,755**	**2,106**	**3,438**	**2,137**	**1,837**	**16,273**	**1,849**
—ESF	5,621	2,048	3,346	2,068	1,837	14,919	1,849
—Other	1,134	58	92	70	0	1,354	0
Humanitarian[c]	**1,656**	**172**	**93**	**80**	**81**	**2,083**	**65**
Department of Defense Programs	**16,072**	**6,339**	**10,001**	**11,946**	**11,532**	**55,890**	**7,159**
Security[d]	**14,570**	**5,813**	**9,558**	**10,996**	**10,582**	**51,518**	**6,155**
—ASFF	13,060	5,607	9,167	10,619	10,200	48,653	5,749
—DOD CN	1,061	206	391	377	382	2,416	405
—Other	450	0	0	0	0	450	0
Governance and development[e]	**1,502**	**527**	**443**	**950**	**950**	**4,371**	**1,004**
—CERP	952	527	443	400	400	2,721	425
—AIF	0	0	0	400	400	800	400
—Other	550	0	0	150	150	850	179
Drug Enforcement Administration	**106**	**19**	**19**	**19**	**19**	**182**	**18**
Total	**$27,774**	**$9,171**	**$14,199**	**$14,654**	**$13,859**	**$79,657**	**$9,747**

Source: GAO analysis of Departments of Defense, Justice, and State data.

Notes: Table 1 does not include funding provided for U.S. military operations in Afghanistan. Totals may not add due to rounding.

[a]INCLE = International Narcotics Control and Law Enforcement. FMF = Foreign Military Financing. Other international affairs security includes International Military Education and Training (IMET); Nonproliferation, Antiterrorism, Demining, and Related Programs (NADR); and Voluntary Peacekeeping (PKO) funds.

[b]ESF = Economic Support Fund. Other international affairs governance and development includes Development Assistance (DA); Global Health and Child Survival (GHCS); Treasury Technical Assistance; and International Organizations and Programs funds.

[c]Humanitarian assistance includes Migration and Refugee Assistance (MRA); Emergency Refugee and Migration Assistance (ERMA); International Disaster Assistance (IDA); Transition Initiatives; Food for Education/Food for Progress; U.S. food assistance programs authorized through Title I (Food for Progress) and Title II (Food for Peace) of the Food for Peace Act (also known as P.L. 480); the Bill Emerson Humanitarian Trust; and section 416(b) food aid funds.

[d]ASFF = Afghan Security Forces Fund. DOD CN = Department of Defense Drug Interdiction and Counter-Drug Activities. Other DOD security includes Train and Equip funds and National Defense Authorization Act (NDAA) Section 1207 transfers.

[e]CERP= Commander's Emergency Response Program. AIF = Afghanistan Infrastructure Fund. Other Department of Defense governance and development include Task Force for Business and Stability Operations (TFBSO) and Afghanistan Freedom Support Act (AFSA) funds.

As shown in figure 4,

- $56.9 billion, more than two-thirds of the allotments, were provided to support Afghanistan's security in areas such as the development of Afghan army and police forces and counternarcotics efforts.

- $20.6 billion, a quarter of the allotments, were provided to support governance and development efforts such as the construction of roads and schools.

- $2.1 billion, the remainder of the allotments, were provided for humanitarian assistance.

Figure 4: Breakout of U.S. Allotments to Support Afghan Reconstruction and Relief, Fiscal Years 2002-2012

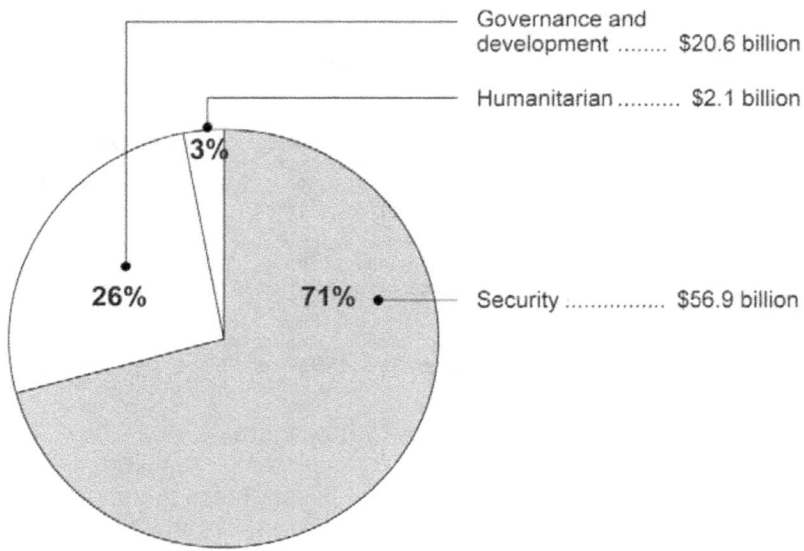

Governance and development .... $20.6 billion

Humanitarian .... $2.1 billion

Security .... $56.9 billion

3%

26%

71%

GAO analysis of Departments of Defense, Justice, and State data.

Recent GAO Work and Recommendations Regarding Afghanistan

Since the issuance of our last Afghanistan key issues product in 2009,[3] we have issued over 50 products and provided numerous congressional briefings on U.S. efforts in Afghanistan. Our work to date has covered key issues outlined in the U.S. strategic framework, including: Afghanistan's security environment, the increase in insider attacks, the transition of security from the United States and NATO to the Afghan government, U.S. efforts to advise and assist the Afghan National Security Forces (ANSF), costs and sustainability of ANSF, DOD planning for the drawdown of forces in Afghanistan, U.S. support for Afghan governance, Afghan donor dependency, U.S. development efforts, and oversight of U.S. contracts and funds, among other issues and concerns. See appendix VI for a list of related GAO products.

---

[3]GAO, *Afghanistan: Key Issues for Congressional Oversight,* GAO-09-473SP (Washington, D.C.: Apr. 21, 2009).

Over the course of our work on U.S. efforts in Afghanistan, we have recommended a range of improvements that should be considered in program planning and implementation and identified conditions that affect success. For example, we have made recommendations on a need for improved interagency coordination and planning, such as the development of plans that include measurable goals, specific time frames, and cost estimates. We have also made recommendations on the need for improved internal controls and oversight over U.S. funds and contracts, such as the provision of adequate training of oversight personnel and completion of preaward risk assessments prior to providing direct assistance to Afghan government ministries. U.S. agencies have generally concurred with our recommendations and have taken steps to address a number of them, several of which are noted in the enclosures. In addition, we have identified several existing conditions—such as the security environment and the limited institutional capacity of the Afghanistan government—that continue to create challenges to the United State's efforts to assist in securing, stabilizing, and rebuilding Afghanistan.

Scope and Methodology of This Review

This special publication represents an update to our April 2009 product, *Afghanistan: Key Issues for Congressional Oversight*, and is based on our work to date. To generate a list of possible key issues, we reviewed past products concerning Afghanistan (as well as the Iraq transition) by GAO, cognizant agency inspectors general (including the Special Inspector General for Afghanistan Reconstruction), the Congressional Research Service, and research institutions. Working with GAO's subject matter experts, we narrowed the list of issues and identified potential oversight questions. We interviewed cognizant agency officials located in Afghanistan and Washington, D.C., from DOD, including U.S. Central Command (CENTCOM), U.S. Forces—Afghanistan (USFOR-A), and U.S. Army Corps of Engineers; North Atlantic Treaty Organization's (NATO) International Security Assistance Force (ISAF); State; the U.S. Agency for International Development (USAID); and the Department of Justice (DOJ), including the Drug Enforcement Administration, Federal Bureau of Investigation, Office of Overseas Prosecutorial Development, Assistance and Training, and International Criminal Investigative Training Assistance Program. We used these interviews to refine our key issues, gain updated information and data, follow up on actions taken regarding our past recommendations, and identify relevant lessons learned from the Iraq transition. We also worked with the officials to determine what portions of our past classified or restricted work could be presented in a public product. We then synthesized this information to provide a balanced and comprehensive overview for each issue and pose oversight questions.

We updated relevant data when possible, and performed additional data reliability assessments when necessary. These additional assessments were only conducted on data that we had not previously reported; all other data were assessed as part of our work to date. We assessed the reliability of the U.S. government budget data for U.S. military operations and reconstruction and relief efforts in Afghanistan by comparing data received from other agencies and asking knowledgeable officials to corroborate and clarify the data.

We updated our estimate of Afghanistan's total public expenditures and converted the data from U.S. fiscal and Afghanistan's solar years to calendar years. To estimate Afghanistan's total public expenditures, we reviewed the government of Afghanistan's budget (revenues, expenditures, and donor contributions) and expenditure data from DOD and State in addition to publicly available expenditure and donor assistance data from the Organization for Economic Cooperation and Development's Development Assistance Database, the World Bank's Afghanistan Reconstruction Trust Fund, United Nations Development Program's Law and Order Trust Fund, India's budget documents, and NATO Training Mission-Afghanistan/Combined Security Transition Command-Afghanistan, among others. Based on our analysis of these documents, we estimated Afghanistan's total public expenditures, on- and off-budget, disaggregated by security and nonsecurity expenditures. Our estimates are based on actual disbursements, not budget estimates. Afghanistan's budget cycle was organized around solar years. For example, solar year 2010/11 begins on March 21, 2010, and ends on March 20, 2011. However, since the latest budget cycle, Afghanistan has switched its reporting to calendar years. We converted Afghanistan's solar year and U.S. fiscal year data by using a quarterly adjustment and assuming a continuous flow of disbursements without quarterly variation.

In most cases, we determined that the data mentioned above were reliable enough for our purposes, and noted our concerns regarding any data reliability issues. The information on foreign law in this report is not the product of our original analysis, but is derived from interviews and secondary sources. Further information on our scope and methodologies, as well as data reliability assessments, can be found in the reports referenced in appendix VI.

We prepared this report under the authority of the Comptroller General to conduct work on GAO's initiative because of broad congressional interest in the oversight and accountability of U.S. funds provided to Afghanistan and to assist Congress with its oversight responsibilities. In addition, Section 1220 of the National Defense Authorization Act for Fiscal Year 2013,[4] requires GAO to report on any substantial updates to the campaign plan for Afghanistan. Appendices IV and V of this report provide an analysis of recent updates to various documents, including the Civil-Military Strategic Framework for Afghanistan, that constitute the strategic framework for U.S. efforts in Afghanistan.[5]

We conducted this performance audit from June 2012 to February 2013 in accordance with generally accepted government auditing standards. Those standards require that we plan and perform the audit to obtain sufficient, appropriate evidence to provide a reasonable basis for our findings and conclusions based on our audit objectives. We believe that the evidence obtained provides a reasonable basis for our findings and conclusions based on our audit objectives.

Agency Comments

We provided a draft of this report for review and comment to DOD, DOJ, State, and USAID. Each agency informed us that they were not providing formal comments. However, each provided technical comments, which we have incorporated into the report where appropriate.

We are sending copies of this report to the appropriate congressional committees. In addition, we are sending copies of this product to the President and Vice President of the United States, and the Secretaries of Defense and State; the Attorney General of the United States, the USAID Administrator; and other interested parties. The report is also available at no charge on the GAO website at http://www.gao.gov. If you or your staff

---

[4]Pub. L. No. 112-239 (Jan. 2, 2013).

[5]In 2012, GAO provided updated information in accordance with its requirements under section 1226 of the National Defense Authorization Act for Fiscal Year 2010 (Pub. L. No.111-84 [October 28, 2009]), focusing on the progress of U.S. civilian-military plans to transition lead security responsibility to the Afghan government (GAO-12-598C), the cost of sustaining the Afghan National Security Forces (GAO-12-438SU), and Afghanistan's donor dependency (GAO-11-948R). These reports are cited in Appendix VI.

have any questions about this report, please contact Charles Michael Johnson, Jr. at (202) 512-7331 or johnsoncm@gao.gov, or the individual(s) listed at the end of each enclosure. Contact points for our Offices of Congressional Relations and Public Affairs may be found on the last page of this product. GAO staff who made key contributions to this product are listed in appendix VII.

Loren Yager
Managing Director
International Affairs and Trade

Janet St. Laurent
Managing Director
Defense Capabilities and Management

Enclosures

List of Addressees

The Honorable Carl Levin
Chairman
The Honorable James M. Inhofe
Ranking Member
Committee on Armed Services
United States Senate

The Honorable Patty Murray
Chairman
The Honorable Jeff Sessions
Ranking Member
Budget Committee
United States Senate

The Honorable Robert Menendez
Chairman
The Honorable Bob Corker
Ranking Member
Committee on Foreign Relations
United States Senate

The Honorable Thomas R. Carper
Chairman
The Honorable Tom Coburn
Ranking Member
Committee on Homeland Security and Governmental Affairs
United States Senate

The Honorable Patrick J. Leahy
Chairman
The Honorable Lindsey Graham
Ranking Member
Subcommittee on State, Foreign Operations, and Related Programs
Committee on Appropriations
United States Senate

The Honorable Howard P. "Buck" McKeon
Chairman
The Honorable Adam Smith
Ranking Member
Committee on Armed Services
House of Representatives

The Honorable Ed Royce
Chairman
The Honorable Eliot L. Engel
Ranking Member
Committee on Foreign Affairs
House of Representatives

The Honorable Darrell E. Issa
Chairman
Committee on Oversight and Government Reform
House of Representatives

The Honorable Kay Granger
Chairman
The Honorable Nita Lowey
Ranking Member
Subcommittee on State, Foreign Operations, and Related Programs
Committee on Appropriations
House of Representatives

The Honorable Jason Chaffetz
Chairman
The Honorable John F. Tierney
Ranking Member
Subcommittee on National Security
Committee on Oversight and Government Reform
House of Representatives

Accountability * Integrity * Reliability

Enclosure I: Afghanistan's Security Environment

Page 17 GAO-13-218SP Afghanistan

Background

Afghanistan's security environment continues to undermine the Afghan government's and international community's reconstruction efforts. In December 2009, recognizing that the situation in Afghanistan had become more grave, the U.S. President announced his decision to deploy additional troops to Afghanistan to disrupt and defeat extremists. In June 2011, the U.S. President announced that combat troops would be withdrawn in 2014.

Afghanistan's Security Situation Remains Volatile

Issue

Several factors have contributed to Afghanistan's current high-threat security environment, challenging the international community and Afghan efforts to implement programs throughout the country. For example, insurgents continue to find safe havens in Pakistan from which to launch attacks. Additionally, the illicit drug trade in Afghanistan continues to be a source of funding for insurgent groups and undermine the Afghan government's effort to improve political stability, economic growth, and rule of law. More recent issues include an increase in attacks on U.S. and coalition personnel by Afghan National Security Forces (ANSF) commonly referred to as "insider attacks," as well as the required transition of some security responsibilities from private contractors to a state-led enterprise—known as the Afghan Public Protection Force (APPF).

Key Findings

The security situation in Afghanistan, as measured by enemy-initiated attacks, has deteriorated since 2005, affecting U.S. and allied reconstruction operations. DOD attack data as of December 2012 show that the pattern of enemy-initiated attacks has remained seasonal in nature, generally peaking from June through September each year and then declining during the winter months (see fig. 5).

Figure 5: Average Daily Enemy-Initiated Attacks Reported by Type in Afghanistan, December 2005 through December 2012

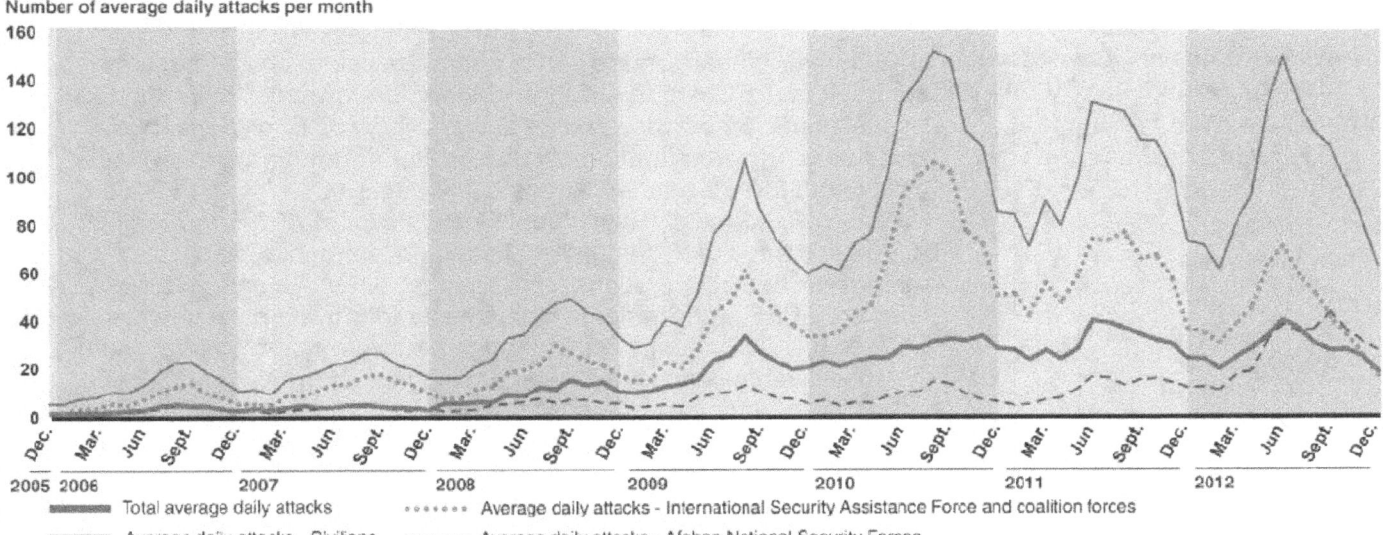

Source: analysis of Defense Intelligence Agency data.

Insider Attacks on U.S. Military Personnel Have Increased

Insider attacks on U.S. and coalition military personnel have increased, raising questions about efforts to protect U.S. personnel working with ANSF. One of the central tenets of the NATO-led International Security Assistance Force (ISAF) mission in Afghanistan is enhanced unit partnering in which coalition units provide training, assistance, and development functions to ANSF units until they are able to conduct operations independently. However, between 2007 and 2012, ANSF killed or wounded over 290 U.S. and international coalition personnel in 87 attacks. The number of these attacks has increased over time (see fig. 6). Among the attacks with identified causes, DOD and NATO have identified the personal motivations of individual ANSF members—including stress and ideological beliefs of attackers with no previous ties to insurgents—as the largest single cause of insider attacks. According to one ISAF and several DOD officials, as the United States and ISAF continue to shift their focus from a combat to an all advise-and-assist mission, larger numbers of personnel may be exposed to a possible insider attack.

Figure 6: Number of Insider Attacks from 2007 through 2012

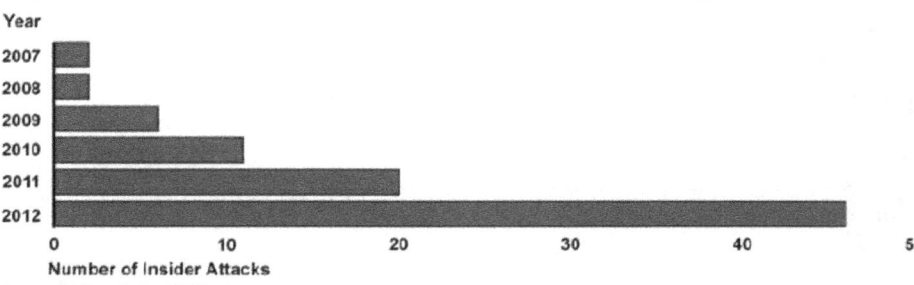

Number of Insider Attacks

Source: GAO analysis of DOD data.

In April 2012, we reported on DOD's increased efforts to reduce the number of insider attacks, but also identified a lack of sharing between DOD and the Afghan government of biometric data (such as fingerprints, iris scans, and facial photographs) that is used to help screen ANSF members before they come into contact with DOD personnel. We recommended that DOD take additional steps to renew the sharing of biometric data on ANSF members and candidates with Afghanistan. DOD agreed with and is making efforts to address our recommendation. Partially because of the increased frequency of insider attacks, ISAF reduced some partnering missions between ISAF and ANSF for a period in September 2012 while new safety protocols were implemented.

NATO and Afghanistan are shifting from the use of private security contractors (PSCs) to the Afghan government-owned APPF, and this transition may affect the security of the military, U.S. civilians, and implementing partners attempting to deliver development assistance throughout the country. An August 2010 decree by Afghan President Karzai directed the dissolution of PSCs in favor of APPF, to provide a fee-for-service force to secure international, governmental, and nongovernmental operations, sites, and facilities. According to U.S. officials, APPF faces various impediments to providing security services to DOD and USAID and its implementing partners, including an immature logistics system, limited recruiting, training and command and control capabilities, equipment shortages, and a lack of qualified English speakers. These impediments could affect APPF operational capabilities and the transition at ISAF sites to APPF protection, and may result in increased security costs, among other things.

The Introduction of the Afghan Public Protection Force May Increase Security Concerns for U.S. Military and Civilian Operations

Points of Contact

For more information, contact:
Charles Michael Johnson, Jr., (202) 512-7331,
johnsoncm@gao.gov
Cary Russell, (202) 512-5431,
russellc@gao.gov

Oversight Questions

1. What is the status of DOD's efforts to reduce the number of insider attacks, such as renewing biometric data sharing with the Afghan government?

2. With the implementation of APPF, what are the effects on security for U.S. agencies and their implementing partners and the cost of providing that security in Afghanistan?

G A O
Accountability * Integrity * Reliability

Enclosure II: Transition of Lead Security to Afghan Security Forces

Background

Since 2001, the United States and its NATO partners have been responsible for securing Afghanistan and leading the effort to secure, stabilize, and rebuild Afghanistan. In 2010, the United States and the international community announced their intentions to transition security to the Afghan government. This transition is under way and is expected to be completed by the end of 2014.

Transition of Lead Security from ISAF to ANSF Is a Joint ISAF-Afghan Process

Issue

In November 2010, the Afghan government and NATO agreed upon a plan for transferring lead security responsibilities from the NATO-led International Security Assistance Force (ISAF) to the Afghan National Security Forces (ANSF) by the end of 2014 with the drawdown of international forces. Specifically, the Afghan government and ISAF—including the United States—agreed to a transition process that emphasizes a shift in ISAF's role from conducting combat missions to advising and assisting ANSF. Lead security responsibility in Afghanistan is defined as responsibility and accountability for planning and conducting operations within a designated area, with ISAF support as required. For example, ANSF continues to rely on coalition forces for, among others, air, logistics, intelligence, and medical evacuation support. The successful transfer of lead security responsibility from international forces to ANSF is critical to countering insurgents and creating sustainable security and allows the withdrawal of international troops.

Key Findings

The transfer of lead security responsibility from ISAF to ANSF is a joint ISAF-Afghan decision-making process that is under way. Under this process, ISAF and Afghan officials determine the readiness of geographic areas to transition based on the following four factors:

1. the capability of ANSF to take on additional security tasks with less assistance from ISAF;
2. the level of security needed to allow the population to pursue routine daily activities;
3. the degree of development of local governance; and
4. whether ISAF is properly positioned to withdraw as ANSF capabilities increase and threat levels diminish.

The transition for each geographic area is a multiphased process, with ISAF tracking progress through metrics, such as security and governance. The areas (provinces, districts, and/or cities) are grouped into one of five tranches for transition. As of December 2012, the transition of four of the five tranches had been announced, and over 87 percent of the Afghan population was living in areas under Afghan lead security with the military support of U.S. and coalition partners. By mid-2013, it is expected that all areas will have entered the transition process and that by December 2014 the transition will be complete.

According to ISAF, ANSF would need to be under effective Afghan civilian control and fully capable of addressing security challenges on a sustainable and irreversible basis for the transition to be successful. However, the readiness of the Afghan government to sustain ANSF has been questioned. For example, we previously highlighted concerns raised about the cost to sustain ANSF (see encl. III). Additionally, in October 2012, the Special Inspector General for Afghanistan Reconstruction (SIGAR) reported that the Afghan government would likely be incapable of fully sustaining ANSF facilities after the transition (SIGAR. *ANSF*

ANSF Capabilities Have Reportedly Increased, but the Tool Used to Assess ANSF Performance Has Changed

ISAF's Mission Is Evolving from Combat to Advise-and-Assist

Points of Contact

For more information, contact:

Charles Michael Johnson, Jr., (202) 512-7331, johnsoncm@gao.gov

Sharon L. Pickup, (202) 512-9619, pickups@gao.gov

Facilities: Concerns with Funding, Oversight, and Sustainability for Operations & Maintenance. Washington, D.C.: Audit 13-1, Oct. 30, 2012).

DOD and ISAF have reported progress in increasing ANSF capabilities, but the tool they use to assess the performance of ANSF units changed several times. When we reported on Afghan National Army capability in January 2011, the highest capability rating level for a unit was "independent," meaning that it could execute the full spectrum of its mission without any assistance from coalition forces. As of August 2011, however, the highest level had changed to "independent with advisors," meaning that a unit could execute its mission, but could also request coalition forces when necessary (see GAO-12-951T). Under these lower standards, more units have been rated at the highest level. In November 2012, DOD reported progress in increasing the capability of ANSF, with 14 percent of army and 13 percent of police units rated at the highest level of capability. In addition, DOD reported that 43 percent of army and 19 percent of police units were rated at the second highest level, "effective with advisors." DOD acknowledged that the changes to the rating levels, as well as the elimination of certain requirements for validating units, were partly responsible for the increase in ANSF units rated at the highest level.

As part of the overall transition of lead security, NATO's mission in Afghanistan is shifting from a combat role to an advise-and-assist mission. For the U.S. contribution, DOD has used a variety of approaches to provide U.S. forces to carry out the advise-and-assist mission. For example, in early 2012, the U.S. Army and Marine Corps began to deploy small teams of advisors with specialized capabilities—referred to as Security Force Assistance Advisory Teams—that are located throughout Afghanistan, to work with Afghan army and police units from the headquarters to the battalion level, and advise them in areas such as command and control, intelligence, and logistics. More recently, the Army began tailoring the composition and mission of its brigade combat teams to further focus on advising efforts. The Army and Marine Corps, however, have continued to face some challenges when supplying these teams, such as in providing the required field grade officers and specialized capabilities. Our past work examining the use of advisor teams in Iraq and Afghanistan highlighted certain areas that we believe are relevant to DOD's plans to provide the Security Force Assistance Advisory Teams in support of the current mission in Afghanistan. Specifically, we have identified challenges related to the sourcing and training of personnel, command-and-control relationships, and support. Given the key role of advisory teams in supporting the transition process, these areas will be important considerations for DOD as it continues to refine its use of advisor personnel to mentor and develop ANSF.

Oversight Questions

1. What is the status of the transition process in those areas where ANSF has taken the lead in security?

2. Given the changing measures of ANSF capabilities, to what extent is ANSF capable of addressing security challenges on a sustainable basis?

3. What enabling capabilities, including advisor support, will DOD need to continue to provide to ANSF beyond 2014?

4. What steps is DOD taking to address challenges in providing advisor personnel, in terms of number of teams, ranks, and specialized capabilities?

G A O
Accountability * Integrity * Reliability

Enclosure III: Future Cost and Sustainability of Afghan Security Forces

Background

An international coalition of countries, including the United States, other NATO members, and other nations, has made contributions to build ANSF, which consists primarily of the Afghan National Army (ANA) and the Afghan National Police (ANP). U.S. agencies allotted over $52 billion to build and sustain ANSF from fiscal years 2002 through 2012.

Afghanistan's Domestic Revenue Will Not Cover the Expected Cost of Its Security Forces

The United States and the International Community Committed to Fund ANSF, but a Funding Gap Is Anticipated

Issue

Helping Afghanistan build capable and sustainable security forces is critical to the success of transitioning lead security responsibilities to Afghanistan by the end of 2014. At the Chicago Summit in May 2012, the international community pledged to continue to assist in financing the sustainment of Afghan National Security Forces (ANSF) beyond 2014. The World Bank, the Afghan government, and the International Monetary Fund (IMF) have reported that Afghanistan will likely need donor assistance to fund ANSF until at least 2021. DOD requested $5.7 billion to support ANSF for fiscal year 2013, which, if approved, would bring the total U.S. funding levels for ANSF for fiscal years 2002 through 2013 to over $57 billion. In Chicago, the Afghan government and the international community agreed with setting a goal for Afghanistan to assume full financial responsibility for its security forces no later than 2024.

Key Findings

Our analysis shows that projected Afghan domestic revenues will be insufficient to cover the cost of ANSF through fiscal year 2015. Our analysis of DOD data estimates that the cost of continuing to build and sustain ANSF will be at least $25 billion for fiscal years 2013 through 2017. Multiple factors are expected to influence the final cost of sustaining ANSF, including the size of the force—which is expected to decline, according to a preliminary model, from 352,000 to 228,500 by 2017—as well as planned reductions in infrastructure and training costs by 2014. According to DOD, continuous efforts are made to adjust ANSF capabilities and requirements to achieve cost reductions, including the Afghan First (the purchase of goods and services from Afghan producers) and Afghan Right (building and procuring items according to Afghan specifications) initiatives. At the Chicago Summit, the Afghan government pledged to devote at least $500 million in 2015 and annually thereafter to funding ANSF, which is about 14 percent of its 2015 projected domestic revenues. However, even if the Afghan government committed 100 percent of its projected domestic revenues to funding ANSF, this amount would cover only about 75 percent of the cost of supporting security forces in fiscal year 2015 and would leave the Afghan government no revenues to cover any non-security-related programs, such as public health.

At the Chicago Summit, the United States and its allies laid out a plan for future funding for ANSF; the U.S. annual contribution is projected to decline over time but still cover the majority of the costs. Our analysis shows that donors funded about 95 percent ($33.7 billion) of Afghanistan's total security expenditures, with the United States funding approximately 91 percent ($32.4 billion) of that amount from 2006 through 2011. On the basis of projections of U.S. and other donor support for ANSF for fiscal years 2012 through 2017, we estimate that there will be a gap each year from 2015 through 2017 between ANSF costs and donor pledges if additional contributions are not made (see fig. 7). According to State, excluding Afghan and U.S. funds, the international community has pledged over $1 billion annually to support ANSF from 2015 through 2017.

Figure 7: Projected U.S. and Other Donor Support for ANSF[a]

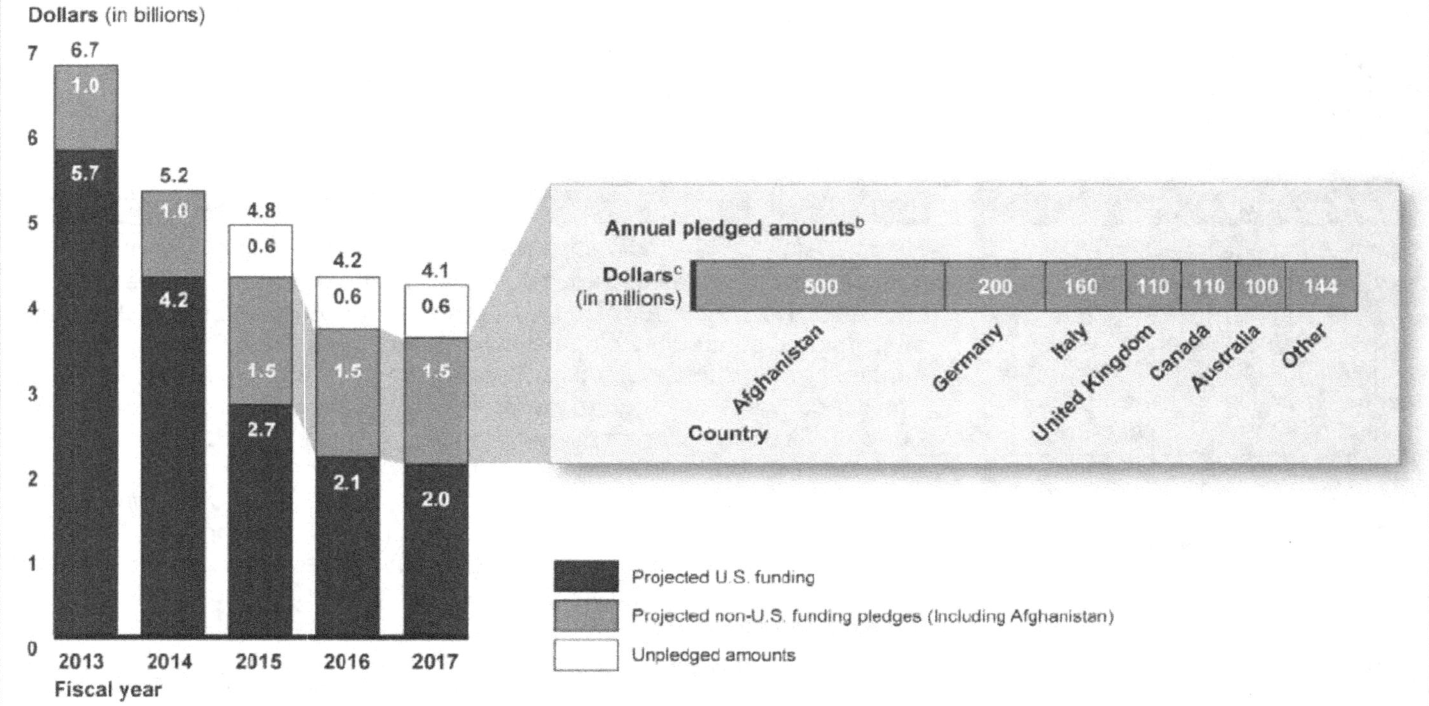

Source: GAO analysis of Departments of Defense and State data.

[a]These projections are based on data and planning assumptions from early 2012 and, according to DOD officials, are subject to change based on ongoing planning efforts to develop and sustain ANSF force structures.

[b]GAO analysis of the projected costs of ANSF is completed by fiscal year, while annual pledged amounts by individual countries are based on calendar year.

[c]Pledges were converted to U.S. dollars using January 24, 2013 currency exchange rates.

Despite Mandate, Long-Term Cost Estimates for Sustaining ANSF Have Not Been Routinely Provided to Congress

Although DOD has developed ANSF cost estimates beyond 2014, it has not provided its long-term cost estimates for sustaining ANSF in its semiannual reports to Congress. Our analysis of DOD data estimates the cost of continuing to support ANSF from 2013 through 2017 over $25 billion, raising concerns about the sustainability of ANSF. We previously recommended, and Congress mandated, that DOD report to Congress about the long-term cost to sustain ANSF. While DOD's semiannual reports issued to date include information on current or upcoming fiscal year funding requirements for ANSF and donor contributions, estimates for long-term costs are absent. DOD stated that because the long-term ANSF cost estimates depend on a constantly changing operational environment, it provides cost information to Congress through briefings and testimony, as appropriate. This mechanism, however, does not allow for independent assessment of DOD's estimates to assist Congress as it considers future budget decisions.

Oversight Questions

1. If the ANSF force size does not decrease as expected, what are the alternative cost estimates and sources of funding for a larger force?

2. To what extent are the United States and the international community identifying additional cost savings for ANSF?

3. To what extent have the United States and the international community developed plans to cover possible ANSF funding gaps?

Points of Contact

For more information, contact:

Charles Michael Johnson, Jr.,
(202) 512-7331,
johnsoncm@gao.gov

GAO
Accountability * Integrity * Reliability

Enclosure IV: DOD Planning for the Drawdown of Equipment in Afghanistan

Background

In June 2011, the United States announced plans to reduce the number of U.S. troops in Afghanistan in accordance with U.S. objectives to transition to an Afghan-led security presence by 2014. DOD completed the reduction of 33,000 troops from Afghanistan in September 2012, but much equipment has accumulated in the country through 10 years of inflow without corresponding outflow.

DOD Has Applied Some Lessons Learned from Iraq to Planning for the Drawdown of Equipment in Afghanistan

DOD Established Command Structures and Guidance, Property Accountability, and Transportation Options for the Drawdown of Equipment in Afghanistan

Issue

With the U.S. military drawdown from Afghanistan, DOD faces an unprecedented logistical challenge. Removing equipment from Afghanistan requires transiting routes with physical and geopolitical challenges. These factors could increase costs and slow the drawdown of an estimated 50,000 vehicles and more than 90,000 containers. DOD has begun planning for the reduction of hundreds of thousands of major end items—that is, equipment important to operational readiness such as aircraft, motorized and towed vehicles, and weapons—worth more than $36 billion. To drawdown the major end items, DOD has three primary options: remove the equipment from Afghanistan; transfer it to another agency or to the Afghan government; or destroy it in-theater. According to one DOD estimate, the cost of removal and transfer of items could be almost $6 billion. Senior DOD officials who oversaw the logistics for the military withdrawal from Iraq see a greater challenge in Afghanistan.

Key Findings

DOD has applied some, but not all, relevant lessons learned from the Iraq drawdown to its planning for equipment reductions in Afghanistan. For example, the drawdown from Iraq demonstrated the importance of early planning for equipment drawdown, and the military services have applied this lesson by issuing guidance outlining the processes and procedures for drawing down equipment in Afghanistan. However, not all lessons from the Iraq drawdown have been applied. For example, during the Iraq drawdown, the Army noted that contractor equipment should be inventoried and entered into an automated records accounting system. However, DOD officials told us that full inventory of contractor equipment has not yet been attained in Afghanistan. In September 2011, we recommended that DOD implement a process to maintain visibility over contractor equipment. At the time, DOD agreed with the recommendation.

DOD has planned for the reduction of equipment from Afghanistan in the following three ways, but challenges remain:

(a) *Established command structures and guidance.* DOD's Central Command designated U.S. Forces-Afghanistan (USFOR-A) as the command responsible for equipment drawdown. USFOR-A has published a base closure and transfer guide that outlines processes for the handling of equipment during transition.

(b) *Made efforts to improve property accountability.* In September 2011, USFOR-A initiated an inventory of all the equipment in Afghanistan to identify items not previously accounted for in DOD's systems of record, but DOD officials acknowledged that they lack visibility over contractor equipment.

(c) *Established and expanded transportation options.* DOD has increased the capacity of air/sea transportation routes out of Afghanistan (see fig. 8), but the land/sea routes from Afghanistan have limited operational capability for the return of equipment. U.S. Transportation Command is currently conducting tests to determine the capacity of the land/sea routes for the return of equipment from Afghanistan. Because of geopolitical complexities in the region it is unknown when these land/sea routes will be operational for the removal of equipment. As a result, DOD has had to rely on a combination of air/sea transport, a more costly transportation option.

DOD transportation costs for the return of equipment vary depending on such factors as the type of equipment, route, and mode of transportation. For example, according to DOD data, transportation costs for the return of a single vehicle or container can range from $8,000 to $153,000, depending on the option employed (see fig. 8).

Figure 8: Cost of Various Routes for the Removal of Containers and Vehicles from Afghanistan

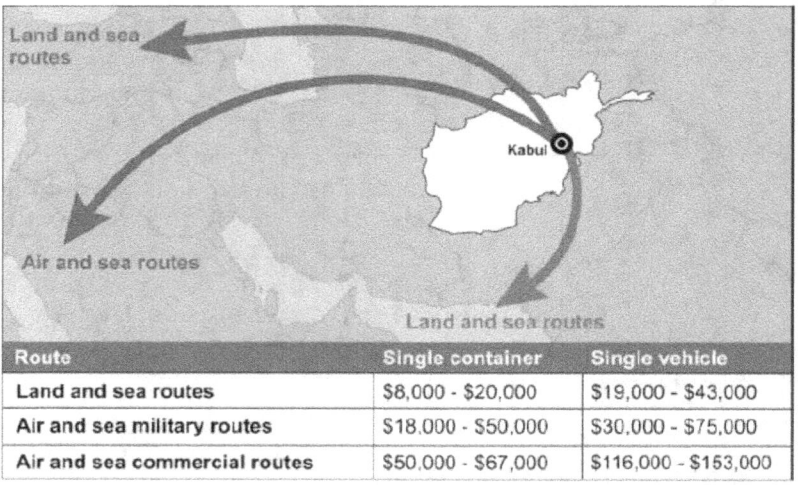

Route	Single container	Single vehicle
Land and sea routes	$8,000 - $20,000	$19,000 - $43,000
Air and sea military routes	$18,000 - $50,000	$30,000 - $75,000
Air and sea commercial routes	$50,000 - $67,000	$116,000 - $153,000

Source: GAO analysis of DOD data.

DOD Has Not Fully Considered the Costs and Benefits of Returning Excess Equipment from Afghanistan

Consistent with DOD's supply chain materiel management policy, DOD has issued additional guidance requiring the military services to assess and document the costs and benefits when equipment is transferred or destroyed. However, there is no specific guidance requiring the military services to assess and document the costs and benefits of returning equipment, and they have not done so. Returning equipment involves transportation, repair, and storage costs that could be weighed against benefits to determine whether it is actually cost-effective to return it. Based on our analysis, the return of these items without full consideration of the costs and benefits is particularly problematic for unneeded items. When such excess items are returned without full consideration of costs and benefits, there is increased risk of unnecessary transportation and storage expenditures. In December 2012, we recommended that the military services conduct and document analyses to compare the costs and benefits of returning excess items and use these analyses in decisions regarding their return (see GAO-13-185R). DOD concurred.

Oversight Questions

1. To what extent does DOD's execution of the equipment drawdown support drawdown objectives and milestones with an efficient use of resources?

2. To what extent has DOD developed mitigation plans to address potential cost and operational impacts for removing equipment if there are disruptions to land-based supply routes?

3. To what extent do decision makers have sufficient information on the costs and benefits of returning excess items?

Point of Contact

For more information, contact:

Cary Russell, (202) 512-5431, russellc@gao.gov

Enclosure V: Afghanistan's Donor Dependence

G A O
Accountability * Integrity * Reliability

Background

Afghanistan is one of the world's poorest countries and ranks near the bottom of virtually every development indicator category. The nation's gross domestic product (GDP) is estimated at about $18 billion for 2011. According to the most recent figures, approximately 35 percent of Afghanistan's population is unemployed and lives below the poverty line, suffering from shortages of housing, clean drinking water, and electricity.

Afghanistan's Domestic Revenues Do Not Cover Its Total Public Expenditures

The United States and International Partners Funded about 90 Percent of Afghanistan's Estimated Total Public Expenditures

Issue

The international community, including approximately 50 countries and international entities such as the World Bank and the United Nations, has provided significant support to help stabilize and rebuild Afghanistan. U.S. agencies have allotted over $81.7 billion for reconstruction and relief in Afghanistan between fiscal years 2002 and 2012, and the U.S. President has requested over $9.7 billion for these purposes for fiscal year 2013. In July 2012, at the international conference in Tokyo, Japan, donor countries and international organizations committed to continue supporting the Afghan economy through 2015 and beyond. Donors also raised concerns about Afghanistan's dependency on donors to fund its public expenditures—funds spent to provide public services to the Afghan population, such as security, infrastructure projects, and government salaries—and continued reconstruction efforts. We have raised concerns about Afghanistan's inability to fund planned government expenditures without foreign assistance (see GAO-11-948R).

Key Findings

Afghanistan's domestic revenues funded about 10 percent of its estimated total public expenditures from 2006 to 2011. Domestic revenue grew from $0.6 billion to $2.0 billion from 2006 to 2011 (see fig. 9), an increase of over 230 percent. At the same time, Afghanistan's estimated total public expenditures grew from $5.8 billion to $17.4 billion, an increase of over 200 percent, maintaining a gap between revenues and expenditures.

Figure 9: Afghanistan's Domestic Revenues from 2006 to 2011

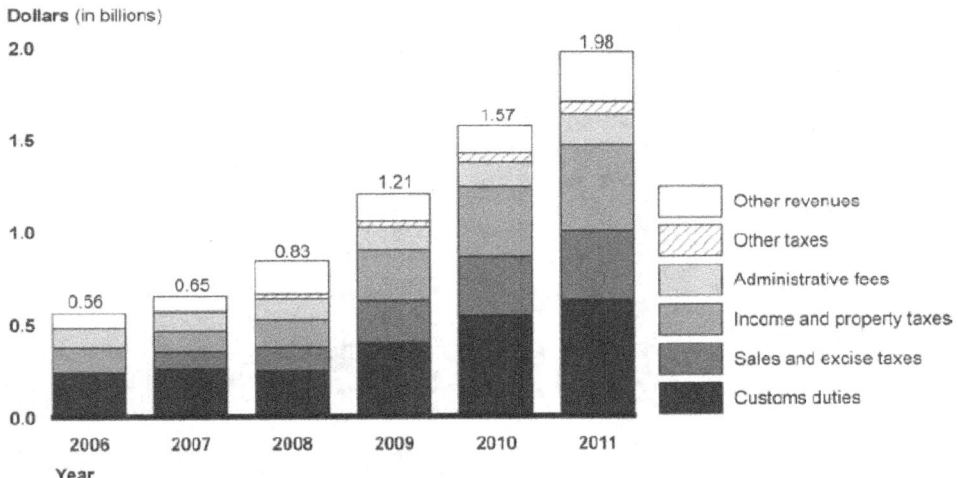

Source: GAO analysis of data from Afghanistan Financial Management Information System (AFMIS).

Donors funded approximately 90 percent of Afghanistan's estimated total public expenditures from 2006 to 2011, with the United States providing 64 percent of that amount (see fig. 10). The United States funded an estimated 91 percent of Afghanistan's total security expenditures and about 37 percent of Afghanistan's total nonsecurity expenditures between 2006 to 2011. In numerous reports and congressional briefings, we have raised concerns about Afghanistan's inability to fund planned government expenditures without foreign assistance and raised questions about the sustainability of U.S.-funded road, agriculture, and water infrastructure development projects, as well as Afghanistan's ability to sustain its national security forces.

Figure 10: Afghanistan's Total Public Expenditures from 2006 to 2011

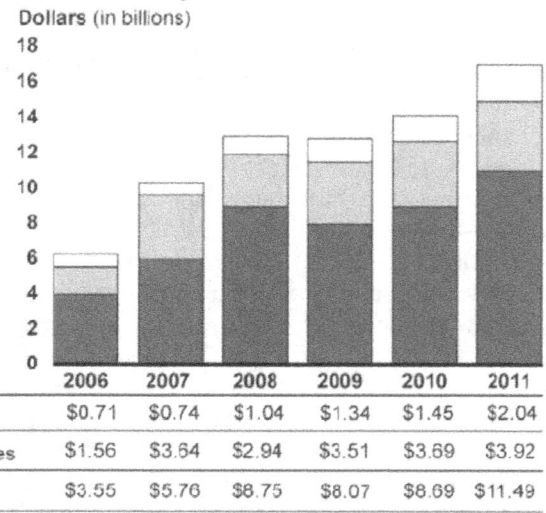

Dollars (in billions)

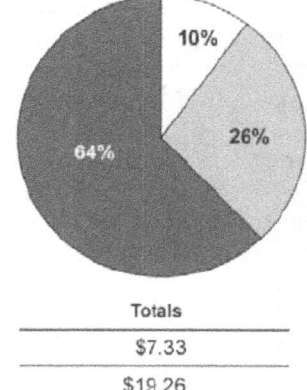

	2006	2007	2008	2009	2010	2011	Totals
Afghan funded expenditures	$0.71	$0.74	$1.04	$1.34	$1.45	$2.04	$7.33
Other donor funded expenditures	$1.56	$3.64	$2.94	$3.51	$3.69	$3.92	$19.26
U.S. funded expenditures	$3.55	$5.76	$8.75	$8.07	$8.69	$11.49	$46.30
Total public expenditures	$5.81	$10.14	$12.73	$12.92	$13.83	$17.44	$72.89

Source: GAO analysis of Afghan, U.S. agencies, and other donor data.

Note: Numbers may not add due to rounding.

Donors Funded Over Half of Afghanistan's On-Budget Expenditures and All Off-Budget Expenditures

Donors funded, on average, 56 percent of Afghanistan's on-budget expenditures and 100 percent of its off-budget expenditures. Between 2006 and 2011 about 79 percent of Afghanistan's estimated $73 billion in total public expenditures were "off-budget"—that is, funded by the international community outside of the Afghan national budget, such as equipment for Afghan National Security Forces. The remaining expenditures were "on-budget"—that is, within the government's budget and funded by domestic revenues and donor contributions. As a result, a majority of Afghanistan's total public expenditures were outside the direct control of the Afghan government.

International Community Has Pledged Continued Support

The international community has pledged to continue to support Afghanistan through 2017 if certain metrics regarding reform in Afghanistan are met. Given Afghanistan's future revenue generation projections and expenditures, the country will likely continue to be reliant on the donor community through at least 2024. In July 2012, the international community committed to providing over $16 billion for Afghanistan's economic development through 2015. The community also committed to sustaining support, through 2017, at or near the levels of the past decade to respond to the fiscal gap estimated by the World Bank and the Afghan government.

Oversight Questions

1. To what extent are U.S. programs assisting Afghanistan's ability to increase domestic revenue and close the gap between revenues and total public expenditures?

2. What is the estimated amount of U.S. and other donors' financial contributions to Afghanistan expected to be through 2017?

Points of Contact

For more information, contact:

Charles Michael Johnson, Jr., (202) 512-7331, johnsoncm@gao.gov

Accountability * Integrity * Reliability

Enclosure VI: Oversight and Accountability of U.S. Funds to Support Afghanistan

Background

Since 2002, U.S. agencies have collectively allotted over $80 billion to help stabilize Afghanistan and build the Afghan government's capacity to provide security, enhance governance, and develop a sustainable economy. The United States provides assistance to Afghanistan through contracts and assistance instruments, such as grants and cooperative agreements, and in the form of direct assistance, or "on-budget" assistance—funding provided through the Afghan national budget for use by its ministries.

U.S. Efforts to Improve Afghanistan's Financial Management Capacity Continue

Issue

In 2010, the United States pledged to provide at least 50 percent of its development aid through the Afghan government budget within 2 years. Such direct assistance is intended to help develop the capacity of Afghan government ministries. The United States more than tripled its awards of such direct assistance to Afghanistan in fiscal year 2010 compared with fiscal year 2009, using bilateral agreements and multilateral trust funds. Improving the Afghan government's management of public finances is critical to the successful transition of more development aid being provided though the Afghan government budget. According to U.S. officials and documents, a challenge to this effort is the high level of corruption that exists throughout the Afghan government. Persistent corruption in Afghanistan undermines security and the people's belief in the government, as well as effective accountability of U.S. funds provided directly to the Afghan government.

Key Findings

The United States continues to make efforts to improve Afghanistan's public financial management capacity to develop a budget, expend funds, and increase accountability and transparency. For example, the U.S. Agency for International Development (USAID) and the Departments of the Treasury and Defense (DOD) have supported the Afghan government's goals to improve its capacity to develop a national budget and expend funds through various activities, such as USAID projects that provide technical assistance and training to Afghan civil servants. A number of factors, however, including high levels of corruption in Afghanistan, pose ongoing challenges to these programs.

We found in 2011 that U.S. government efforts were aligned with Afghan government goals; however, the U.S. government could not fully determine the overall extent to which its efforts had improved the Afghan government's public financial management capacity because (1) U.S. agencies have reported mixed results; and (2) weaknesses in USAID's performance management frameworks, such as lack of performance targets and data, prevent reliable assessments of its results (see GAO-11-907). In September 2011 we recommended that for public financial management efforts USAID take steps to establish performance targets in its Mission Performance Management Plan (PMP) and ensure that implementing partners' PMPs include baselines and approved targets, among other recommendations. In November 2011, USAID approved the contractor's updated performance management plan for its only remaining public financial management capacity project to include baseline and targets for each indicator. Addressing concerns about the capacity of Afghan officials to administer larger amounts of funding for development and public services programs is important, as more donor funding is expected to be provided directly to Afghanistan's budget in 2013 and beyond.

USAID and DOD have taken steps to help ensure the accountability of
their direct assistance to Afghan ministries. In 2011, although we found
that USAID had established and generally complied with various financial
and other controls in its direct assistance agreements (such as requiring
Afghan ministries to maintain separate bank accounts and records subject
to audit), it had not always assessed the risks in providing direct
assistance before awarding funds (see GAO-11-710). For example,
USAID had not completed preaward risk assessments in two of the eight
cases of bilateral assistance we identified, despite the USAID
administrator's prior commitment to Congress that the agency would not
proceed with direct assistance to an Afghan public institution before
assessing its capabilities. USAID has since taken steps to respond to our
recommendations to address these issues, including issuing new agency
policies on risk assessments. We also found that DOD had established
procedures in 2011 governing its direct assistance to Afghan ministries,
following our discussions with DOD about our initial findings.

Figure 11: U.S. Dollars and Afghan Afghanis

Source: GAO and DOD.

To provide a higher level of accountability for U.S. and international
assistance funds, the Afghan government and the international community
agreed at the Tokyo Conference in 2012 to implement accountability
mechanisms including the Mutual Accountability Framework, which was
designed to ensure that the Afghan government is achieving governance
and development goals. Going forward, the Afghan government and the
international community are expected to monitor performance in five major
areas of governance and development and determine a time line for
achieving Framework goals. Additionally, following the Tokyo Conference,
the Afghan President presented an anticorruption decree enumerating
specific actions that the Afghan government will take to improve
governance and the rule of law.

A Mutual Accountability
Framework Designed to
Improve Accountability of U.S.
and International Funds to
Afghanistan Is to Be
Implemented

Oversight Questions

1. What steps have U.S. agencies taken to help ensure that
    anticorruption efforts in Afghanistan will enhance accountability of U.S.
    funds in Afghanistan?

2. To what extent is the Afghan government prepared to handle higher
    levels of direct assistance, given the capacity challenges faced
    throughout the government?

3. To what extent is the Mutual Accountability Framework designed to be
    effective in ensuring that the Afghan government is achieving
    governance and development goals?

G A O
Accountability * Integrity * Reliability

Enclosure VII: Oversight and Streamlining of Development Assistance to Afghanistan

Background

The United States has devoted significant funding and efforts in Afghanistan to development activities and programs. Its strategic framework identifies socio-economic development as a key pillar of achieving its objectives of countering insurgent activity in Afghanistan.

Oversight of U.S. Programmatic Development Funds Has Been Enhanced

U.S. Development Efforts in Afghanistan Overlap and May Duplicate Each Other

Issue

U.S. agencies have allotted almost $20 billion for development efforts in Afghanistan since 2002 through the U.S. Agency for International Development (USAID) and the Departments of Defense (DOD) and State (State). These agencies have undertaken thousands of development activities in Afghanistan through multiple programs and accounts. In a number of cases, however, systemic weaknesses in oversight and monitoring of development project and program performance in Afghanistan exist, and the various programs and accounts used to execute development activities in Afghanistan overlap to some degree across categories of development assistance. While such overlap could be beneficial in terms of synergy and unity of effort, it also creates the potential for duplication of efforts if plans and activities are not properly coordinated.

Key Findings

Oversight of the billions of dollars provided to U.S. development programs in Afghanistan has been enhanced. We have previously reported on systemic weaknesses in USAID's oversight and monitoring of the performance of projects and programs carried out by its implementing partners in Afghanistan. In 2010 we reported that USAID did not consistently follow its established performance management and evaluation procedures with regard to its agriculture and water sector projects. For example, only two of the seven USAID-funded agricultural programs included in our prior review had targets for all of their performance indicators. We concluded that, in the absence of consistent application of its existing performance management and evaluation procedures, USAID's programs were more vulnerable to corruption, waste, fraud, and abuse. In response to our recommendations to improve its performance oversight and monitoring, USAID took several steps including issuing a new performance monitoring plan and approving its implementing partners performance targets.

The four main U.S. development programs and accounts in Afghanistan have similar goals and activities, overlap to some degree, and may duplicate each other's efforts (see table 1 for a description of those programs and accounts). Programs administered by USAID and DOD funded similar activities in Afghanistan across similar, broadly defined categories of assistance: agriculture, democracy and governance, education and health, energy and electricity, economic growth, and transportation. We found in fiscal year 2011 that these programs were implemented in many of the same Afghan provinces and districts—in 33 of the 34 provinces and in 249 of the 399 districts (see GAO-13-34). According to agency officials, these overlapping development efforts can be beneficial, provided that agencies leverage their respective expertise and coordinate efforts. However, the officials also acknowledged that such overlap creates the potential for duplication of efforts if plans and activities are not properly coordinated.

Table 2: Major U.S.-Administered Programs or Accounts Used to Fund Development Efforts in Afghanistan

	Economic Support Fund (ESF)	Commander's Emergency Response Program (CERP)[a]	Task Force for Business and Stability Operations (TFBSO)	Afghanistan Infrastructure Fund (AIF)
Primary agency or agencies responsible	USAID	DOD	DOD	DOD and State
Fiscal year in which funding for Afghanistan began	2002	2004	2009	2011
Program or account description for Afghanistan	Supports Afghan government in its efforts to promote economic growth, establish a democratic and capable state governed by the rule of law, and provide basic services for its people.	Enables U.S. commanders in Afghanistan to carry out small-scale projects designed to meet urgent humanitarian relief and reconstruction needs in their areas of responsibility.	Supports projects to help reduce violence, enhance stability, and support economic normalcy through strategic business and economic opportunities.	Supports high-priority, large-scale infrastructure projects that support the U.S. civilian-military effort in Afghanistan.
Funding provided in fiscal year 2011 (millions)[b]	$2,068	$400	$224	$400
Total funding provided since inception (millions)[b]	$14,919	$3,439	$555	$800

Source: GAO analysis of Office of Management and Budget and agency data.

[a]CERP may also fund some nondevelopment activities. We exclude nondevelopment CERP activities from our analyses in this table.

[b]Funding is based on allocations and agency allotments for Afghanistan assistance.

U.S. Agencies Use Various Methods to Coordinate but Lack a Shared Database That Includes All Development Efforts

U.S. agencies use a variety of methods to coordinate development efforts in Afghanistan, but lack a single database to share and retain data. Our analysis of USAID's development activities and DOD's CERP activities identified potentially duplicative development projects; however, we could not conclusively determine whether or not these efforts had resulted in duplication (providing the same goods and services to the same beneficiaries) because of gaps and inconsistencies in USAID's and DOD's respective databases. USAID and DOD officials cited informal communication and interagency meetings as the primary method of coordinating USAID and CERP efforts. However, the effectiveness of such coordination may depend on the priorities of the staff involved and could be hampered by high staff turnover and lack of data retention.

In 2010 we recommended that agencies report their development efforts in a shared database; however, agencies have made limited progress in collecting and retaining critical data on development efforts in such a database. USAID's Afghan Info database has been designated as the central repository of data for U.S. foreign assistance efforts in Afghanistan. DOD has not reported its projects in the shared database, citing concerns with the sensitive nature of its data, which USAID noted could be mitigated by internal controls. We continue to believe that a shared database that incorporates all U.S.-funded development efforts in Afghanistan, including DOD's CERP activities, is needed to help mitigate potential information-sharing gaps and reduce the risk of duplication. In November 2012 we asked Congress to consider requiring U.S. agencies to report information on their development-related activities in a shared database. While USAID agreed with this recommendation citing concerns about visibility into DOD projects post-2014, DOD disagreed with the need for legislative action.

Points of Contact

For more information, contact:

Charles Michael Johnson, Jr., (202) 512-7331, johnsoncm@gao.gov

Oversight Questions

1. What steps are U.S. agencies taking to ensure that USAID has insight into DOD projects?

2. What steps have U.S. agencies taken to develop a shared database that includes all development efforts?

Enclosure VIII: Oversight of U.S. Contracts in Afghanistan

Background

DOD, State, and USAID have relied extensively on contractors to support troops and civilian personnel and conduct reconstruction efforts in Afghanistan. For fiscal year 2012, DOD obligated approximately $17.6 billion on contracts performed in Afghanistan, with State and USAID reporting obligations of $633 million and $714 million, respectively.

Contract Management during the Drawdown and Transition Requires Continued Attention

Oversight of U.S. Contracts Requires Additional Improvement

Issue

Since 2001, contractors have played a key role in U.S. efforts to stabilize and rebuild Afghanistan. Federal agencies have hired contractors to increase agricultural capacity, train Afghan police, maintain weapons systems, and provide security and logistical services to U.S. forces and other personnel. As the United States moves forward with planning for the drawdown of U.S. military forces and the transition to a civilian-led presence in Afghanistan, the Department of Defense (DOD) needs to plan for the efficient demobilization of its contractors, while the Department of State (State) needs to conduct acquisition planning for contract support after the transition. At the same time, DOD, State, and the U.S. Agency for International Development (USAID) continue to face contract and management challenges, such as ensuring that a sufficient number of trained personnel are available to oversee contractors and that vendors and contractor personnel are vetted effectively.

Key Findings

DOD's and State's experiences in Iraq highlight important considerations for contract management that require continued attention during the drawdown and transition to a civilian-led presence in Afghanistan. During the drawdown from Iraq, DOD faced challenges with demobilizing its contractors, including determining contract requirements and identifying risks associated with potential changes in contracting vehicles. We made several recommendations in April 2010 to address related concerns, which DOD took steps to address. Additionally, as occurred in Iraq, the ratio of contractor to military personnel may increase substantially as the drawdown progresses in Afghanistan, as contractors provide some services previously provided by military personnel. This relative growth in contractor personnel as the pool of military personnel available to perform contract oversight functions decreases necessitates an increased focus on oversight to help mitigate the risk of fraud, waste, and abuse.

Furthermore, as we reported in August 2012, coordination between DOD and State occurred late during the Iraq drawdown, contributing to delays that made the transition and associated acquisitions of critical goods and services more challenging. State found itself without sufficient personnel with the expertise to conduct necessary acquisition activities to support its mission in Iraq, and, as a result, relied on DOD for acquisition support. However, the departments did not fully comply with requirements for the use and management of such support, which continues to limit State's ability to conduct acquisition planning for the transition in Afghanistan. Over the next year, as the U.S. transition in Afghanistan evolves, the departments face a shrinking window of opportunity to determine whether State's continued reliance on DOD is appropriate or State should develop its own capacity. Otherwise, State risks again relying on DOD's support by default rather than through sound business decisions.

DOD, State, and USAID face contract management and oversight challenges in Afghanistan, and their oversight of U.S. contracts requires additional improvement. For example, as we reported in September 2012, the three agencies continue to experience difficulty in reporting reliable information on their contracts and contractor personnel in Afghanistan. Such information is a starting point for ensuring proper management and oversight. Furthermore, in March 2012, we reported that DOD oversight personnel in Afghanistan did not always receive adequate training and that DOD continued to lack a sufficient number of oversight personnel in Afghanistan, which in some cases resulted in projects being completed without sufficient oversight. In April 2010 we reported that, absent strategic planning for their use of contractors, individual offices within State and USAID often made case-by-case decisions on using contractors to support contract or grant administration, and risks, such as possible conflicts of interest or insufficient oversight, were not always addressed. We recommended that the agencies take actions such as developing new training standards, conducting workforce planning, and issuing relevant guidance. The agencies have taken steps to address some of these recommendations and challenges. For example, DOD has developed a new training course for contract oversight personnel with a focus on contingency operations, while State has developed new guidance to address conflict of interest and contract oversight risks. USAID has also implemented an initiative in Afghanistan that includes several efforts to improve contract award and oversight processes. However, additional efforts will be necessary to help ensure sufficient contract oversight.

Our prior work also identified limitations among DOD's, State's, and USAID's procedures for ensuring that vendors and contractor personnel are vetted effectively to help minimize risks to U.S. efforts and personnel. We reported in June 2011 that DOD and USAID had developed vendor vetting programs in part to address concerns that money from U.S. contracts was being diverted to fund insurgent and criminal activities, but State had not. At that time, we also reported on limitations in procedures for vetting non-U.S. vendors and emphasized the need for better information sharing among agencies about vendor vetting. We recommended that DOD and USAID take steps to improve their vetting processes by using a risk-based approach and that State assess the need for and possible options to vet non-U.S. vendors. We also recommended that the agencies consider procedures to improve information sharing. DOD and USAID have since taken steps to improve their vetting processes, and in June 2012, State announced that it would begin vetting certain contractors in Afghanistan. A concept for an interagency vetting working group to improve information sharing among Embassy sections and agencies has also been developed. Going forward, continued attention will be necessary to help ensure effective vetting processes and procedures in Afghanistan and future contingency operations.

Contractor Vetting Procedures Need Continued Attention

Oversight Questions

1. What steps is DOD taking to plan for its use and demobilization of contractors during its drawdown from Afghanistan?

2. How are DOD and State coordinating for a transition of contracted services when State assumes the lead U.S. role in Afghanistan after the drawdown of U.S. forces?

3. To what extent do DOD, State, and USAID have adequate staff resources, both in terms of numbers and expertise, in Afghanistan to ensure the appropriate level of contract management and oversight?

4. How will DOD, State, and USAID institutionalize lessons learned about contract management in Afghanistan to help ensure that they do not face similar contract management challenges in future contingencies?

Point of Contact

Timothy DiNapoli, (202) 512-4841, dinapolit@gao.gov

Cary Russell, (202) 512-5431, russellc@gao.gov

G A O
Accountability * Integrity * Reliability

Enclosure IX: Planning for the Future U.S. Presence in Afghanistan

Background

In 2001, after the fall of the Taliban, the United States established a diplomatic and military presence in Afghanistan. The total number of U.S. civilians under the authority of the U.S. embassy peaked at 1,253 in January 2012. Civilian personnel under DOD authority reached a high of 3,022 in March 2011, coinciding with the highest number of U.S. troops at 99,800. The United States has since begun to draw down its civilian and military personnel in Afghanistan.

Transition from Military to Civilian-Led Presence in Iraq Could Offer Lessons for Afghanistan

U.S. Civilian Presence in Afghanistan Is Expected to Remain Substantial

Issue

Plans for the United States' post-combat presence in Afghanistan, currently scheduled to begin in January 2015, have been developed by the Departments of State (State) and Defense (DOD) and are currently being reviewed by U.S. National Security Staff. The United States is transitioning from counterinsurgency and stability operations toward more traditional diplomatic and development activities, according to U.S. strategic documents. Current plans envision a diplomatic presence at the U.S. embassy in Kabul and four consulates in other major cities. A possible smaller but continuing military presence in Afghanistan is expected to advise and assist Afghan National Security Forces (ANSF) and continue counterterrorism efforts beyond 2014. Current plans call for a further drawdown of both civilians and military personnel; however, specific figures have not yet been determined.

Key Findings

While the circumstances, combat operations, and diplomatic efforts in Iraq differ from those in Afghanistan, potential lessons can be learned from the transition from a military to civilian-led presence in Iraq and applied to Afghanistan to avoid possible missteps and better utilize resources. In Iraq, State and DOD had to revise their plans for the U.S. presence from more than 16,000 personnel at 14 sites down to 11,500 personnel at 11 sites after the transition had begun—in part because the United States did not obtain the Government of Iraq's commitment to the planned U.S. presence. Given these reductions, we found that State was projected to have an unobligated balance of between about $1.7 billion and about $2.3 billion in its Iraq operations budget at the end of fiscal year 2013. According to DOD officials, U.S. Forces-Iraq planning assumed that a follow-on U.S. military force would be approved by both governments. The decision not to have a follow-on force led to a reassessment of DOD's plans and presence. Attacks on diplomatic facilities in countries such as Libya should also be considered as the United States plans future facilities in Afghanistan. U.S. agencies should take the necessary steps to ensure that all facilities in Afghanistan meet security standards to the maximum extent possible and that mitigating steps are taken to address vulnerabilities. We previously recommended that such steps be taken in Iraq; U.S. agencies concurred and have since begun vulnerability assessments at Iraq sites.

State's current plans for the U.S. civilian presence in Afghanistan call for maintaining a significant presence of diplomats. In May 2012, the U.S. and Afghan Presidents signed a Strategic Partnership Agreement that committed both countries to strengthened long-term strategic cooperation. Additionally, in July 2012, the U.S. President declared Afghanistan a "major non-NATO ally," 1 of 15 countries to receive such status, which qualifies Afghanistan for certain privileges supporting defense and security cooperation. These and other agreements, as well as U.S. planning documents, demonstrate the intention of the United States to maintain strong civilian and diplomatic ties with Afghanistan.

Figure 12: U.S. Embassy in Kabul, Afghanistan

U.S. Embassy Kabul's Chancery as of 2011

U.S. Embassy Kabul's proposed expanded Chancery-estimated completion in November 2014

Source: U.S. Department of State.

State Plans for Five Diplomatic Sites in Afghanistan Post-2014

State's enduring presence plan includes an embassy in Kabul (see fig. 12, above left), and four other posts in, according to State officials, the key strategic locations of Herat, Mazar-e-Sharif, Jalalabad, and Kandahar. The U.S. embassy in Kabul is currently undergoing a major construction project to expand the chancery and replace temporary offices and housing with permanent structures. A new consulate facility in Herat opened in March 2012. Although State determined that the initially selected site for a consulate facility in Mazar-e-Sharif was found to be unsuitable, a new location has not yet been decided upon. To date, State has committed approximately $900 million to expand embassy facilities and establish new consulate facilities in Herat and Mazar-e-Sharif. Additional costs to establish consulate facilities in Jalalabad and Kandahar have not yet been determined. According to officials, State is planning for over 700 civilians to be posted in Afghanistan beyond 2014. All plans, according to State officials, are subject to ongoing deliberations.

Future U.S. Military Presence in Afghanistan Is Uncertain

Although U.S. and Afghan officials have stated that a continued military partnership between the two countries is desired beyond 2014, the details of that partnership have not yet been determined. Sensitive issues on the status and precise nature of an ongoing U.S. military presence remain to be negotiated between the United States and Afghanistan. U.S. and Afghan authorities began negotiations on a bilateral security agreement in November 2012 to establish a framework for the U.S. military's post-2014 presence. As agreed in the May 2012 Strategic Partnership Agreement, the goal is to complete the negotiations of the bilateral security agreement within one year, by November 2013. This agreement is expected to supersede the current status of forces agreement upon entry into force. According to DOD officials, issues regarding the future roles and responsibilities of any U.S. forces that remain in Afghanistan after 2014, such as immunity for foreign military forces under Afghan law, are likely to present a challenge as negotiations progress.

Point of Contact

For more information, contact:

Charles Michael Johnson, Jr., (202) 512-7331, johnsoncm@gao.gov

Sharon L. Pickup, (202) 512-9619, pickups@gao.gov

Oversight Questions

1. In light of the lessons learned from the Iraq transition, to what extent has State taken steps to plan for the U.S. presence in Afghanistan?

2. What steps are State and DOD taking to ensure that all post-2014 facilities meet security guidelines and that site vulnerabilities are addressed?

3. What steps has the United States taken to plan for the multiple possible outcomes of the bilateral security agreement negotiations?

Appendix I: Key Facts about Afghanistan

Figure 13: Key Facts about Afghanistan

INSTRUCTIONS for interactive graphic: Click your mouse here to return to Figure 1.

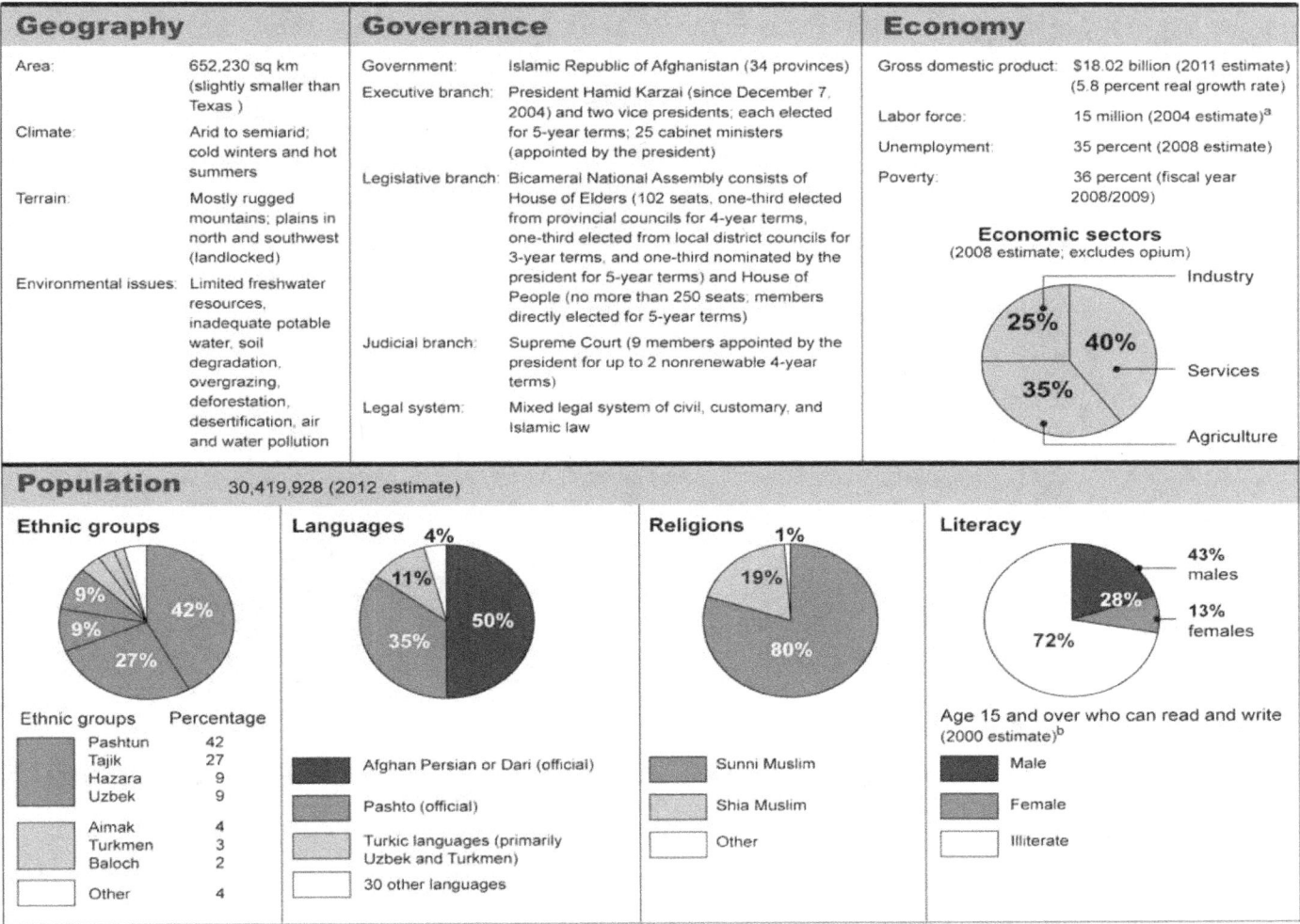

Source: Central Intelligence Agency, The World Factbook, and Government of Afghanistan, *National Risk and Vulnerability Assessment 2007/2008: A Profile of Afghanistan*

[a]Afghanistan's National Risk and Vulnerability Assessment 2007/2008: A Profile of Afghanistan identified a smaller labor force of over 12 million.

[b]Afghanistan's National Risk and Vulnerability Assessment 2007/2008: A Profile of Afghanistan found a lower literacy rate of 26 percent of the total adult population (39 percent for males and 12 percent of females).

Appendix II: Ethnic Map of Afghanistan

Figure 14: Ethnic Map of Afghanistan

INSTRUCTIONS for interactive graphic: Click your mouse here to return to Figure 1.

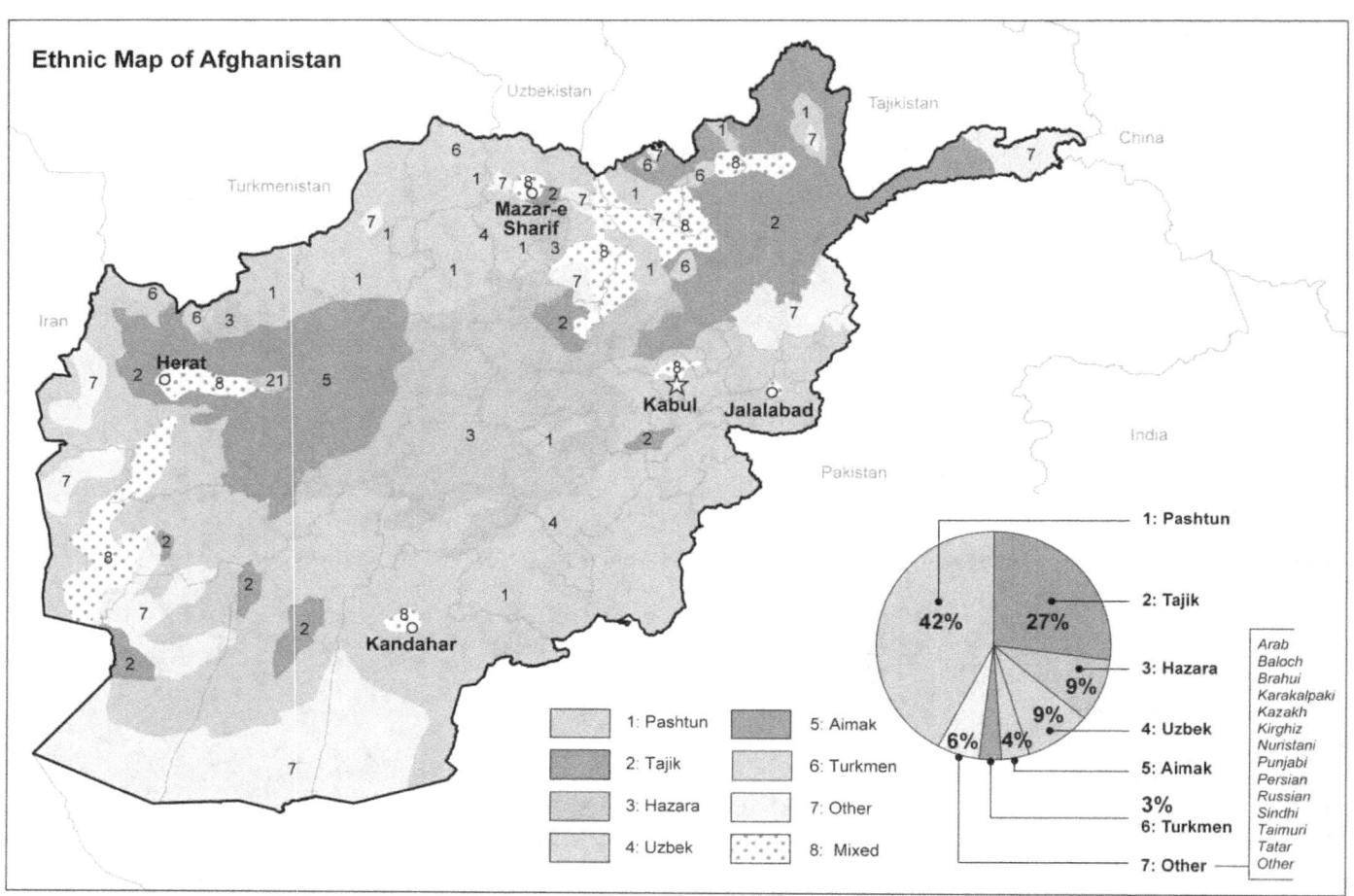

Source: GAO analysis of Central Intelligence Agency and National Geospatial-Intelligence Agency data; National Geospatial-Intelligence Agency and Map Resources (maps).

Appendix III: Major U.S. Transit Points into and out of Afghanistan

Figure 15: Major U.S. Transit Points into and out of Afghanistan

INSTRUCTIONS for interactive graphic: Click your mouse here to return to Figure 1.

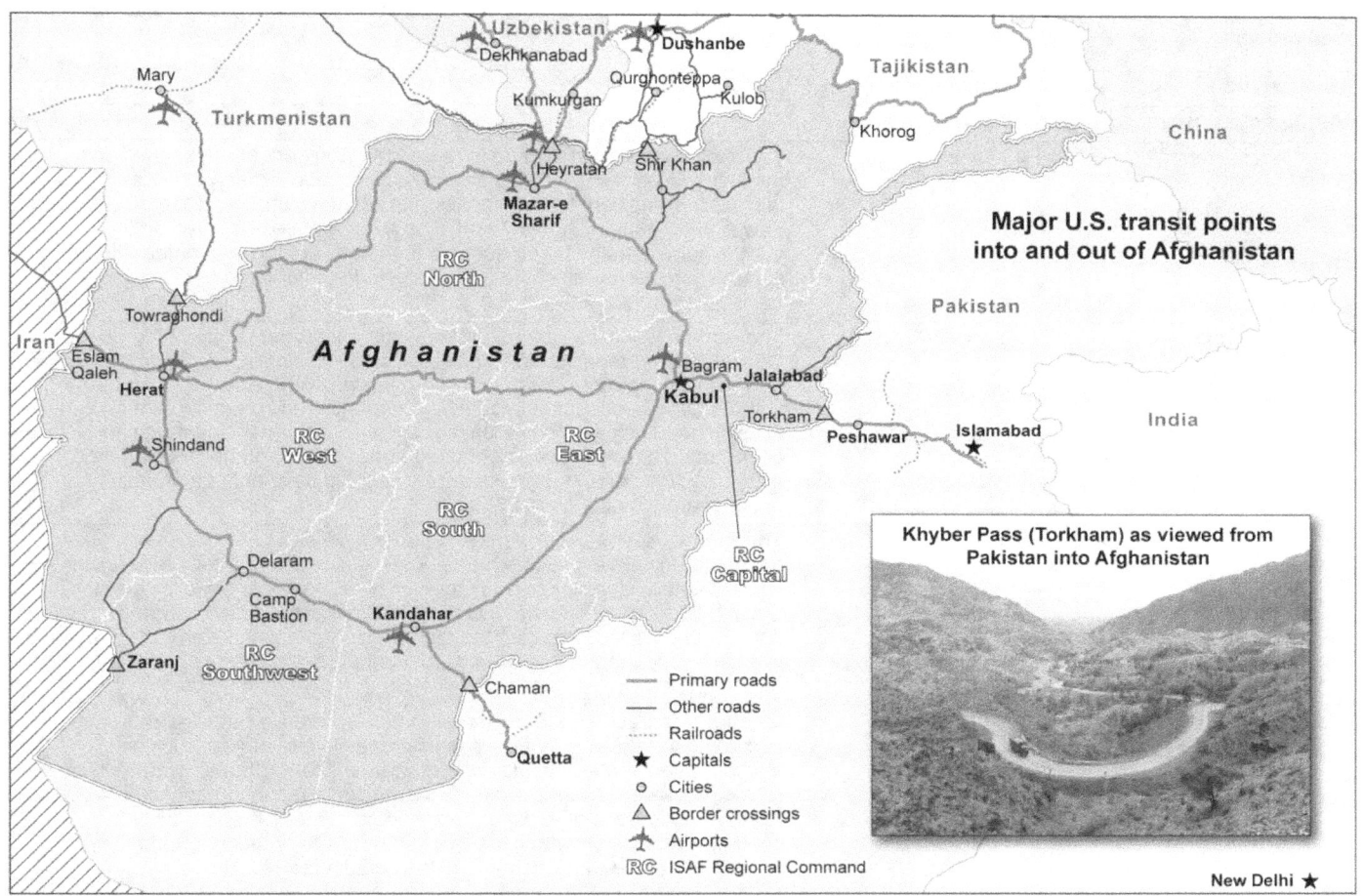

Source: GAO based on USTRANSCOM NGASupport Team NST and Map Resources (map); photograph by James Mollison, August 2004.

Appendix IV: Documents that Constitute the Strategic Framework for U.S. Efforts in Afghanistan

This appendix provides information regarding documents shown in figure 3 (see table 3). This information can also be accessed via the interactive rollovers in the electronic version of the figure.

Table 3: Descriptions of the Afghan, U.S., and NATO Documents that Constitute the Strategic Framework for U.S. Efforts in Afghanistan

Documents	Date issued	Description
Afghan documents and international agreements		
Bonn Agreement	December 2001	The Bonn Agreement, signed in December 2001 under the sponsorship of the United Nations (UN), was the first of several international agreements that laid out a framework for the transition of Afghanistan from Taliban rule to a new Afghan national government. The agreement established an interim authority for Afghanistan, requested the UN to authorize an international security force to assist in the transition, and set out the role of the UN to advise the interim authority.
Afghan Compact	January 2006	The Afghan Compact (January 2006) was the product of the 2006 London Conference—a meeting of Afghanistan's government, over 50 other nations, and the UN and other international organizations. The compact first introduced the concept of security, governance, and development as the areas of focus for Afghan reconstruction activities. In the compact, the Afghan government, with the support of the international community, committed to achieving benchmarks in these areas, such as developing a professional national army by the end of 2010.
Afghan National Development Strategy	2008	The Afghan National Development Strategy (2008) is Afghanistan's guiding document for achieving its reconstruction goals. The strategy focuses on improving the country's security, governance, and economic growth and reducing poverty. It also provides information on the resources needed to carry out the strategy and on the shortfall in Afghanistan's projected revenue. It was released in 2008 and is effective through 2013.
London Conference Communiqué	January 2010	The London Conference Communiqué, issued in January 2010, was the product of the 2010 London Conference. Conference participants committed to helping the government of Afghanistan in several areas, such as anticorruption and improving the capability of the Afghan army and police forces. Conference participants also acknowledged the intention of NATO's North Atlantic Council to begin transitioning the lead responsibility for security—province by province—from NATO's International Security Assistance Force to Afghan forces in late 2010/early 2011.
Kabul Process	July 2010	The Kabul Process, established as a result of the July 2010 Kabul Conference, created an internationally agreed-upon "path to an economically sustainable, socially vibrant and stable Afghanistan, led by Afghans for Afghans, [and] supported by the international community." The Process is defined by the National Priority Programs, which were introduced at the conference and address a wide range of issues raised in the Afghan National Development Strategy and serve as a prioritization and implementation plan for the strategy.

Appendix IV: Documents that Constitute the
Strategic Framework for U.S. Efforts in
Afghanistan

Documents	Date issued	Description
Bonn Conference Conclusions	December 2011	The Bonn Conference Conclusions, issued at the December 2011 Bonn Conference, began the discussion of Afghanistan's future during 2015-2024—which was termed the "Transformation Decade" at the conference—following international declarations that international military forces would complete their drawdown in Afghanistan by December 2014.
Chicago Summit Declaration	May 2012	The Chicago Summit Declaration, issued at the May 2012 Chicago Summit, drew together the 28 NATO countries and Afghanistan to discuss the sustainability of Afghan National Security Forces beyond the drawdown of international military forces in 2014. Nations affirmed their commitment with pledges of financial support.
Enduring Strategic Partnership Agreement	May 2012	The Enduring Strategic Partnership Agreement Between the United States of America and the Islamic Republic of Afghanistan was signed on May 2, 2012. The agreement details several areas in which both parties agree to support one another, including protecting and promoting shared democratic values, advancing long-term security, reinforcing regional security and cooperation, supporting social and economic development, and strengthening Afghan institutions and governance. As part of this agreement, the United States pledged to designate Afghanistan a Major Non-NATO Ally (MNNA), and did so on July 6, 2012; MNNA status qualifies a country for certain privileges supporting defense and security cooperation, but does not entail any security commitments to that country.
Tokyo Conference Declaration and Framework	July 2012	The Tokyo Conference Declaration and Framework, issued at the July 2012 Tokyo Conference, resulted in a declaration of continued support toward Afghanistan's long-term economic growth and fiscal self-reliance, called upon greater Afghan effort to combat corruption, and elicited pledges of financial support for Afghanistan as it heads into the "Transformation Decade." It also introduced the Mutual Accountability Framework that holds Afghanistan and the international community accountable for achieving and supporting good governance goals and indicators across five areas.
U.S. plans and strategies		
Operation Enduring Freedom Campaign Plan	November 2001 continuing	The Operation Enduring Freedom Campaign Plan (2001) and updates are classified. Operation Enduring Freedom is the ongoing U.S.-led operation that coordinates with ISAF to conduct counterterrorism operations in Afghanistan and elsewhere. It operates under a U.S. commander who is also the commanding general of ISAF.
Status of Forces Agreement	May 2003	The Status of Forces Agreement was established through the exchange of diplomatic notes on September 26, December 12, 2002, and May 28, 2003, and entered into force on May 28, 2003. The agreement lays out the status of DOD military and civilian personnel in Afghanistan in connection with cooperative efforts in response to terrorism; humanitarian and civic assistance; military training and exercises; and other activities. These personnel are accorded a status equivalent to administrative and technical staff of the U.S. embassy under the Vienna Convention on Diplomatic Relations of 1961, making them immune from criminal prosecution by Afghan authorities, among other protections.

Appendix IV: Documents that Constitute the
Strategic Framework for U.S. Efforts in
Afghanistan

Documents	Date issued	Description
Afghanistan and Pakistan Regional Stabilization Strategy	November 2011	The Afghanistan and Pakistan Regional Stabilization Strategy, signed by the Secretaries of Defense and State, was released in January 2010 and, according to State officials, most recently updated in November 2011 through the Status Report: Afghanistan and Pakistan Civilian Engagement. The report focuses on U.S. non-military efforts and states that the U.S. combat mission is not open-ended but that the United States is committed to building a lasting partnership with Afghanistan and Pakistan. With regard to Afghanistan, the strategy focuses on supporting an Afghan-led, sustainable transition; building an economic foundation for Afghanistan's future; supporting Afghanistan's governance and political institutions; strengthening Afghan rule of law; sustainable development investments; advancing the rights of Afghan women and girls; and oversight of Afghanistan assistance. Under each of these areas, the strategy identifies key issues and achievements. According to State officials, it supersedes the March 2009 U.S. Strategy for Afghanistan and Pakistan.
Afghanistan Pakistan Objectives 2015	August 2012	Afghanistan Pakistan Objectives 2015, signed in August 2012, replaced the National Security Council Strategic Implementation Plan signed in July 2009 and is classified. According to State officials, the plan provides a series of goals and objectives for implementing the Afghanistan and Pakistan Regional Stabilization Strategy. The plan also includes measures of effectiveness to track progress in achieving the objectives.
Civil-Military Strategic Framework for Afghanistan	October 2012	The Civil-Military Strategic Framework for Afghanistan was originally signed in August 2009 (and named the Integrated Civilian-Military Campaign Plan) by the U.S. ambassador to Afghanistan and the commanding general, U.S. Forces-Afghanistan. It was updated in February 2011, March 2012, and October 2012 and renamed the Civil-Military Strategic Framework. The current framework is less detailed than the original to be more adaptable and allow flexibility, according to officials. The framework is designed to articulate the strategic vision guiding U.S. government efforts to achieve U.S. national goals in Afghanistan and to ensure that U.S. civilian and military efforts in Afghanistan are fully integrated and complementary. The plan addresses four categories of effort, including security, governance, rule of law, and socioeconomic development, as well as the crosscutting issues of reconciliation and reintegration, the role of women in society, borders, information initiatives, and regional cooperation.
Enduring Presence Plans Post 2014	2012	According to State officials, the Enduring Presence Plans Post 2014 are classified planning documents submitted by State, DOD, and the Intelligence Community to the National Security Staff. Together they lay out initial plans for the post-2014 U.S. presence in Afghanistan.
NATO plans and documents		
Supreme Headquarters of the Allied Powers Europe (SHAPE) Operational Plan	June 2003	The SHAPE OPLAN (June 2003) is a classified document. According to a NATO official, this plan was issued in 2003 to direct NATO operations inside Kabul. SHAPE, a component of NATO, was established in 1951 as part of an effort to establish an integrated and effective NATO military force. SHAPE's mission is to prepare, plan, and conduct military operations in order to meet NATO political objectives.
	August 2012	The SHAPE OPLAN (August 2012) is a classified document. According to a NATO official, this plan provided for NATO to assume responsibility throughout Afghanistan—all regions plus established Regional Command Capital (Kabul). This document was revised three times since its initial release in April 2006.

Appendix IV: Documents that Constitute the
Strategic Framework for U.S. Efforts in
Afghanistan

Documents	Date issued	Description
International Security Assistance Force (ISAF) Operational Plan	March 2006 continuing	The ISAF OPLAN (March 2006) is classified. The current revision was released in October 2011. ISAF is a NATO-led mission in Afghanistan established by the UN Security Council in December 2001. ISAF is composed of troops contributed by the United States, Canada, Australia, New Zealand, and other nations, including member nations of the European Union and NATO. ISAF conducts operations in Afghanistan to reduce the capability and will of the insurgency, support the growth in capacity and capability of the Afghan National Security Forces, and facilitate improvements in governance and socioeconomic development.
NATO Strategic Plan for Afghanistan	May 2012	The NATO Strategic Plan for Afghanistan (May 2012) is classified. According to DOD, it confirms NATO's commitment to Afghanistan through 2024 and defines objectives for ISAF through the completion of security transition at the end of 2014. It also includes a mid-2013 interim milestone for the Coalition and Afghanistan marking the beginning of the ANSF assumption of the lead for combat operations across the country and a shift in NATO's primary mission from combat to training, advising, and assisting in order to ensure the ANSF have required support while adjusting to their increased responsibilities. It replaced the April 2008 Comprehensive Strategic Political Military Plan.
North Atlantic Council Initiating Directive	October 2012	The North Atlantic Council Initiating Directive (October 2012) is classified. According to DOD, the North Atlantic Council acknowledges commitments made at the Chicago summit and issued the North Atlantic Council Initiating Directive to start formal operations planning for the post-2014 NATO-led international training, advisory, and assistance mission in Afghanistan.

Sources: Department of Defense, Department of State, U.S. Mission to NATO, U.S. Special Representative for Afghanistan and Pakistan, U.S. Central Command, U.S. Agency for International Development, UN, and government of Afghanistan documents.

Appendix V: U.S. Civil-Military Strategic Framework for Afghanistan

This appendix provides information regarding the U.S. Civil-Military Strategic Framework for Afghanistan in figure 3. This information can also be accessed via the interactive rollovers in the electronic version of the figure.

Strategic Goal

The U.S. strategic goal for Afghanistan is to disrupt, dismantle, and defeat al Qaeda and prevent its return to Afghanistan and Pakistan. Specific objectives in Afghanistan in support of this goal are to (1) deny safe haven to al Qaeda and (2) deny the Taliban the ability to overthrow the Afghan government.[1]

Pillars and Key Priorities

Each pillar below contains key priorities.

- Security foundation
    - Security is the foundation of the Framework, creating an environment that allows progress on the three key pillars. The counterinsurgency campaign will degrade the insurgency to a level that denies it the ability to threaten the Afghan state and enable the Afghan National Security Forces (ANSF) to assume full responsibility for security by the end of 2014.
    1. Support the development of an increasingly capable ANSF that can partner with the International Security Assistance Force (ISAF) to neutralize the insurgency.
    2. Execute the counterinsurgency campaign.

- Governance pillar
    - Working with the United Nations Assistance Mission to Afghanistan and allied partners, the United States will continue to support Afghan efforts to strengthen governance by facilitating efforts to ensure that government and its institutions are representative, accountable, responsive, constitutionally legitimate, and capable of performing key functions.

---

[1]The U.S. strategic goals for Afghanistan were recently changed from those that appeared in the October 2012 U.S. Civil-Military Strategic Framework for Afghanistan. The goals as they appeared in October 2012 were to (1) disrupt, dismantle, and defeat al Qaeda and its affiliates and prevent their return to Afghanistan; and (2) build a partnership with the Afghan people that ensures that the United States will be able to continue to target terrorists and support a sovereign Afghan government.

1. Support constitutional succession through credible and inclusive presidential elections.

2. Strengthen checks and balances and independent institutions.

3. Strengthen revenue collection and budget prioritization, execution, and accountability at both the national and subnational levels.

4. Stem corruption through support for open and accountable government.

- Rule of law pillar
  - The United States will support Afghan efforts to offer meaningful access to fair, efficient, and transparent justice based on Afghan law. The United States also will support Afghan efforts to increase the government of Afghanistan's legitimacy among Afghans by promoting a culture that values the rule of law. U.S. government rule-of-law entities will continue to pursue a wide range of activities focusing on the fight against corruption in Afghanistan. The U.S. government also will support the government of Afghanistan's efforts to transition the Afghan National Police to a rule-of-law based institution. Collectively, these efforts are expected to form the foundation for a functioning civil society.

1. Increase access to justice by developing institutional capacity, providing legal education, and strengthening capacity to combat corruption.

2. Partner with the government of Afghanistan to increase its capacity to manage a safe, secure, and humane correctional system that discourages the radicalization of prisoners.

3. Provide support for traditional justice systems.

4. Develop law enforcement leadership and capacity.

- Socioeconomic development pillar
  - The United States will support sustainable, inclusive economic growth that will help Afghanistan to be increasingly integrated economically within the region. The United States will also facilitate access between Afghanistan and the international economy to strengthen governmental and private sector development.

1. Support private sector investment, job creation, and food security.

2. Improve Afghanistan's economic integration into the region through the New Silk Road Initiative, which will improve

Afghanistan's ability to access foreign markets and supply its domestic market.

3. Strengthen the capacity of the government of Afghanistan to act as an important enabler of sustainable private sector participation in the economy, regulatory reform, public revenue generation, and improved flow of resources from Kabul to the provinces.

4. Strengthen the capacity of the government of Afghanistan at central and subnational levels to operate and maintain infrastructure and key services, and support critical gains in education and health.

Crosscutting Issues

- *Reconciliation and reintegration:* The United States will continue to support Afghan efforts to achieve a broad-based political reconciliation that includes leadership elements of the insurgency.

- *Role of women in society:* The United States will continue to prioritize gender issues to ensure the positive gains of the last 11 years are irreversible and Afghanistan achieves continued progress on the protection and promotion of women's rights.

- *Borders:* The United States will support government of Afghanistan efforts to improve its border management practices, apply consistently the rule of law, and increase efforts to interdict cross border movement of terrorist, insurgent, and criminal networks, addressing these networks' associated financial activity.

- *Information initiatives:* The United States will pursue the use of strategic communications and access to information for Afghan citizens that support credible and inclusive presidential elections, promote the government of Afghanistan's legitimacy, counter extremist voices, and facilitate transition.

- *Regional cooperation:* The United States is committed to supporting all confidence-building measures outlined in the Kabul Conference, offering support and assistance in a way that makes sense for the region, and is welcomed by the region's countries. For example, the Istanbul Process on Regional Security and Cooperation for a Secure and Stable Afghanistan between Afghanistan and neighboring countries represents an opportunity for the region's countries to develop more cooperative arrangements on security, trade, infrastructure, and natural disasters.

Appendix VI: Related GAO Products

This appendix provides a list of recent products related to each enclosure. Report numbers with an SU or RSU suffix are Sensitive but Unclassified and those with a C suffix are classified.

Sensitive but Unclassified and Classified reports are available to personnel with the proper clearances and need-to-know upon request. For a copy of a Sensitive but Unclassified or Classified report, please contact the point of contact listed in the related enclosure.

Letter

The Strategic Framework for U.S. Efforts in Afghanistan. GAO-10-655R. Washington, D.C.: June 15, 2010.

Afghanistan Security: Multiple Campaign and Operational Plans Direct U.S. Efforts in Afghanistan. GAO-10-619C. Washington, D.C.: June 15, 2010.

Overseas Contingency Operations: Reported Obligations for the Department of Defense. GAO-09-1022R. Washington, D.C.: September 25, 2009.

Overseas Contingency Operations: Reported Obligations for the Department of Defense. GAO-09-791R. Washington, D.C.: July 10, 2009.

Afghanistan: U.S.- and Internationally-Funded Roads (GAO-09-626SP), an E-supplement to GAO-09-473SP. GAO-09-626SP. Washington, D.C.: April 21, 2009.

Afghanistan: Key Issues for Congressional Oversight. GAO-09-473SP. Washington, D.C.: April 21, 2009.

Enclosure I: Afghanistan's Security Environment

Defense Biometrics: Additional Training for Leaders and More Timely Transmission of Data Could Enhance the Use of Biometrics in Afghanistan. GAO-12-442. Washington, D.C.: April 23, 2012.

Afghan Security: Renewed Sharing of Biometric Data Could Strengthen U.S. Efforts to Protect U.S. Personnel from Afghan Security Force Attacks. GAO-12-471SU. Washington, D.C.: April 20, 2012.

Combating Terrorism: U.S. Government Should Improve Its Reporting on Terrorist Safe Havens. GAO-11-561. Washington, D.C.: June 3, 2011.

Drug Control: International Programs Face Significant Challenges Reducing the Supply of Illegal Drugs but Support Broad U.S. Foreign Policy Objectives. GAO-10-921T. Washington, D.C.: July 21, 2010.

Afghanistan's Security Environment. GAO-10-613R. Washington, D.C.: May 5, 2010.

Afghanistan Drug Control: Strategy Evolving and Progress Reported, but Interim Performance Targets and Evaluation of Justice Reform Efforts Needed. GAO-10-291. Washington, D.C.: March 9, 2010.

Afghanistan's Security Environment. GAO-10-178R. Washington, D.C.: November 5, 2009.

Enclosure II: Transition of Lead Security to Afghan Security Forces

Afghanistan Security: Security Transition. GAO-12-598C. Washington, D.C.: September 11, 2012.

Observations on U.S. Military Capabilities to Support Transition of Lead Security Responsibility to Afghan National Security Forces. GAO-12-734C. Washington, D.C.: August 3, 2012.

Afghanistan Security: Long-standing Challenges May Affect Progress and Sustainment of Afghan National Security Forces. GAO-12-951T. Washington, D.C.: July 24, 2012.

Interim Results on U.S.-NATO Efforts to Transition Lead Security Responsibility to Afghan Forces. GAO-12-607C. Washington, D.C.: May 18, 2012.

Security Force Assistance: Additional Actions Needed to Guide Geographic Combatant Command and Service Efforts. GAO-12-556. Washington, D.C.: May 10, 2012.

Intelligence, Surveillance, and Reconnaissance: Actions Needed to Improve DOD Guidance, Integration of Tools, and Training for Collection Management. GAO-12-396C. Washington, D.C.: April 5, 2012.

Afghanistan Security: Department of Defense Effort to Train Afghan Police Relies on Contractor Personnel to Fill Skill and Resource Gaps. GAO-12-293R. Washington, D.C.: February 23, 2012.

Language and Culture Training: Opportunities Exist to Improve Visibility and Sustainment of Knowledge and Skills in Army and Marine Corps General Purpose Forces. GAO-12-50. Washington, D.C.: October 31, 2011.

Iraq and Afghanistan: Actions Needed to Enhance the Ability of Army Brigades to Support the Advising Mission. GAO-11-760. Washington, D.C.: August 2, 2011.

DOD Has Increased Its Use of Intelligence, Surveillance, and Reconnaissance Capabilities in Afghanistan but Would Benefit from Improved Planning for Using Its Capabilities and Utilization of Lessons Learned. GAO-11-224C. Washington, D.C.: February 23, 2011.

Enclosure III: Future Cost and Sustainability of Afghan Security Forces	*Afghanistan Security: Long-standing Challenges May Affect Progress and Sustainment of Afghan National Security Forces.* GAO-12-951T. Washington, D.C.: July 24, 2012. *Afghanistan Security: Estimated Costs to Support Afghan National Security Forces Underscore Concerns about Sustainability.* GAO-12-438SU. Washington, D.C.: April 26, 2012. *Afghanistan Security: Afghan Army Growing, but Additional Trainers Needed; Long-Term Costs Not Determined.* GAO-11-66. Washington, D.C.: January 27, 2011.
Enclosure IV: DOD Planning for the Drawdown of Equipment in Afghanistan	*Afghanistan Drawdown Preparations: DOD Decision Makers Need Additional Analyses to Determine Costs and Benefits of Returning Excess Equipment.* GAO-13-185R. Washington, D.C.: December 19, 2012. *Defense Management: Steps Taken to Better Manage Fuel Demand but Additional Information Sharing Mechanisms Are Needed.* GAO-12-619. Washington, D.C.: June 28, 2012. *Warfighter Support: DOD Has Made Progress, but Supply and Distribution Challenges Remain in Afghanistan.* GAO-12-138. Washington, D.C.: October 7, 2011. *Defense Logistics: DOD Needs to Take Additional Actions to Address Challenges in Supply Chain Management.* GAO-11-569. Washington, D.C.: July 28, 2011.

Iraq Drawdown: Opportunities Exist to Improve Equipment Visibility, Contractor Demobilization, and Clarity of Post-2011 DOD Role. GAO-11-774. Washington, D.C.: September 16, 2011.

Warfighter Support: Preliminary Observations on DOD's Progress and Challenges in Distributing Supplies and Equipment to Afghanistan. GAO-10-842T. Washington, D.C.: June 25, 2010.

Warfighter Support: Preliminary Observations on DOD's Progress and Challenges in Distributing Supplies and Equipment to Afghanistan. GAO-10-462C. Washington, D.C.: March 4, 2010.

Operation Iraqi Freedom: Actions Needed to Facilitate the Efficient Drawdown of U.S. Forces and Equipment from Iraq. GAO-10-376. Washington, D.C.: April 19, 2010.

Operation Iraqi Freedom: Preliminary Observations on DOD Planning for the Drawdown of U.S. Forces from Iraq. GAO-10-179. Washington, D.C.: November 2, 2009.

Enclosure V: Afghanistan's Donor Dependence	*Afghanistan's Donor Dependence.* GAO-11-948R. Washington, D.C.: September 20, 2011.
	Afghanistan: Actions Needed to Improve Accountability of U.S. Assistance to Afghanistan Government. GAO-11-710. Washington, D.C.: July 20, 2011.
Enclosure VI: Oversight and Accountability of U.S. Funds to Support Afghanistan	*Afghanistan: USAID Oversight of Assistance Funds and Programs.* GAO-12-802T. Washington, D.C.: June 6, 2012.
	Afghanistan Governance: Performance-Data Gaps Hinder Overall Assessment of U.S. Efforts to Build Financial Management Capacity. GAO-11-907. Washington, D.C.: September 20, 2011.
	Afghanistan: Actions Needed to Improve Accountability of U.S. Assistance to Afghanistan Government. GAO-11-710. Washington, D.C.: July 20, 2011.

Enclosure VII: Oversight and Streamlining of Development Assistance to Afghanistan	*Afghanistan Development: Agencies Could Benefit from a Shared and More Comprehensive Database on U.S. Efforts.* GAO-13-34. Washington, D.C.: November 7, 2012.
	Afghanistan: USAID Oversight of Assistance Funds and Programs. GAO-12-802T. Washington, D.C.: June 6, 2012.
	Foreign Police Assistance: Defined Roles and Improved Information Sharing Could Enhance Interagency Collaboration. GAO-12-534. Washington, D.C.: May 9, 2012.
	DOD Task Force for Business and Stability Operations: Actions Needed to Establish Project Management Guidelines and Enhance Information Sharing. GAO-11-715. Washington, D.C.: July 29, 2011.
	Afghanistan Development: U.S. Efforts to Support Afghan Water Sector Increasing, but Improvements Needed in Planning and Coordination. GAO-11-138. Washington, D.C.: November 15, 2010.
	Afghanistan Development: USAID Continues to Face Challenges in Managing and Overseeing U.S. Development Assistance Programs. GAO-10-932T. Washington, D.C.: July 15, 2010.
	Afghanistan Development: Poverty and Major Crop Production (GAO-10-756SP), an E-Supplement to GAO-10-368. GAO-10-756SP. Washington, D.C.: July 14, 2010.
	Afghanistan Development: Enhancements to Performance Management and Evaluation Efforts Could Improve USAID's Agricultural Programs. GAO-10-368. Washington, D.C.: July 14, 2010.
	Afghanistan and Pakistan: Oversight of U.S. Interagency Efforts. GAO-09-1015T. Washington, D.C.: September 9, 2009.
	Military Operations: Actions Needed to Improve Oversight and Interagency Coordination for the Commander's Emergency Response Program in Afghanistan. GAO-09-615. Washington, D.C.: May 18, 2009.
Enclosure VIII: Oversight of U.S. Contracts in Afghanistan	*Operational Contract Support: Sustained DOD Leadership Needed to Better Prepare for Future Contingencies.* GAO-12-1026T. Washington, D.C.: September 12, 2012.

Iraq and Afghanistan: Agencies Are Taking Steps to Improve Data on Contracting but Need to Standardize Reporting. GAO-12-977R. Washington, D.C.: September 12, 2012.

Iraq and Afghanistan: State and DOD Should Ensure Interagency Acquisitions Are Effectively Managed and Comply with Fiscal Law. GAO-12-750. Washington, D.C.: August 2, 2012.

Contingency Contracting: Agency Actions to Address Recommendations by the Commission on Wartime Contracting in Iraq and Afghanistan. GAO-12-854R. Washington, D.C.: August 1, 2012.

Operational Contract Support: Management and Oversight Improvements Needed in Afghanistan. GAO-12-290. Washington, D.C.: March 29, 2012.

Iraq Drawdown: Opportunities Exist to Improve Equipment Visibility, Contractor Demobilization, and Clarity of Post-2011 DOD Role. GAO-11-774. Washington, D.C.: September 16, 2011.

Iraq and Afghanistan: DOD, State, and USAID Cannot Fully Account for Contracts, Assistance Instruments, and Associated Personnel. GAO-11-886. Washington, D.C.: September 15, 2011.

Operational Contract Support: Actions Needed to Address Contract Oversight and Vetting of Non-U.S. Vendors in Afghanistan. GAO-11-771T. Washington, D.C.: June 30, 2011.

Afghanistan: U.S. Efforts to Vet Non-U.S. Vendors Need Improvement. GAO-11-355. Washington, D.C.: June 8, 2011.

Contingency Contracting: Observations on Actions Needed to Address Systemic Challenges. GAO-11-580. Washington, D.C.: April 25, 2011.

Iraq and Afghanistan: DOD, State, and USAID Face Continued Challenges in Tracking Contracts, Assistance Instruments, and Associated Personnel. GAO-11-1. Washington, D.C.: October 1, 2010.

Operation Iraqi Freedom: Actions Needed to Facilitate the Efficient Drawdown of U.S. Forces and Equipment from Iraq. GAO-10-376. Washington, D.C.: April 19, 2010.

Contingency Contracting: Improvements Needed in Management of Contractors Supporting Contract and Grant Administration in Iraq and Afghanistan. GAO-10-357. Washington, D.C.: April 12, 2010.

Warfighter Support: DOD Needs to Improve Its Planning for Using Contractors to Support Future Military Operations. GAO-10-472. Washington, D.C.: March 30, 2010.

Iraq and Afghanistan: Agencies Face Challenges in Tracking Contracts, Grants, Cooperative Agreements, and Associated Personnel. GAO-10-509T. Washington, D.C.: March 23, 2010.

Warfighter Support: Continued Actions Needed by DOD to Improve and Institutionalize Contractor Support in Contingency Operations. GAO-10-551T. Washington, D.C.: March 17, 2010.

Contingency Contracting: Further Improvements Needed in Agency Tracking of Contractor Personnel and Contracts in Iraq and Afghanistan. GAO-10-187. Washington, D.C.: November 2, 2009.

Contingency Contracting: DOD, State, and USAID Continue to Face Challenges in Tracking Contractor Personnel and Contracts in Iraq and Afghanistan. GAO-10-1. Washington, D.C.: October 1, 2009.

Contingency Contract Management: DOD Needs to Develop and Finalize Background Screening and Other Standards for Private Security Contractors. GAO-09-351. Washington, D.C.: July 31, 2009.

Enclosure IX: Planning for the Future U.S. Presence in Afghanistan	*Iraq and Afghanistan: State and DOD Should Ensure Interagency Acquisitions Are Effectively Managed and Comply with Fiscal Law.* GAO-12-750. Washington, D.C.: August 2, 2012.

Mission Iraq: State and DOD Have Not Finalized Security and Support Capabilities. GAO-12-759RSU. Washington, D.C.: July 26, 2012.

Mission Iraq: State and DOD Face Challenges in Finalizing Support and Security Capabilities. GAO-12-856T. Washington, D.C.: June 28, 2012.

"Status of Transition to State-Led U.S. Security Assistance to Iraq." Sensitive but Unclassified Briefing for Job Code 320893, Washington, D.C.: April 2012.

Afghanistan: Improvements Needed to Strengthen Management of U.S. Civilian Presence. GAO-12-285. Washington, D.C.: February 27, 2012.

Appendix VII: GAO Contact and Staff Acknowledgments

GAO Contact	Charles Michael Johnson, Jr., (202) 512-7331 or johnsoncm@gao.gov
Staff Acknowledgments	In addition to the contact named above, Hynek Kalkus (Assistant Director), Thomas Costa, Julia Jebo Grant, Christopher J. Mulkins, Debbie Chung, Gergana Danailova-Trainor, Etana Finkler, David W. Hancock, Brandon L. Hunt, Guy LoFaro, Anne McDonough-Hughes, Sharon Pickup, Jeremy Sebest, Stephen K. Woods, and Amanda G. Weldon made key contributions to this product. Godwin M. Agbara, Ashley G. Alley, Pedro Almoguera, Johana R. Ayers, Carole F. Coffey, Teakoe Coleman, Aniruddha Dasgupta, Martin de Alteriis, Timothy J. DiNapoli, Mark Dowling, Emily Gupta, Kasea Hamar, Patrick Hickey, Jordan Holt, Farahnaaz Khakoo-Mausel, Joseph Kirschbaum, Bruce Kutnick, Drew Lindsey, Judith A. McCloskey, Tet Miyabara, Mary E. Moutsos, Marcus Lloyd Oliver, Nina Pfeiffer, Elizabeth Repko, Kendal B. Robinson, Luis E. Rodriguez, Cary B. Russell, Mona Sehgal, Esther Toledo, Pierre Toureille, and Sally Williamson provided technical assistance and additional support.

www.ingramcontent.com/pod-product-compliance
Lightning Source LLC
Chambersburg PA
CBHW080544290526
45790CB00006B/2545